SHAPE SHIFTING
The Guitarist's Guide to Mastering the Fretboard

David Brewster

To access audio visit:
www.halleonard.com/mylibrary

Enter Code
4696-9324-2654-0581

ISBN 978-1-57424-371-0
SAN 683-8022

Cover by James Creative Group
Photography by Katie Smith

Copyright © 2020 CENTERSTREAM Publishing
P.O. Box 17878 - Anaheim Hills, CA 92817

www.centerstream-usa.com | centerstrm@aol.com | 714-779-9390

All rights for publication and distribution are reserved.
No part of this book may be reproduced in any form or by any Electronic or mechanical means including information storage and retrieval systems without permission in writing from the publisher, except by reviewers who may quote brief passages in review.

Special Thanks

A big thanks go out to my family and friends, including all of my Facebook friends and fiends.

Table of Contents

About the Author 4

Introduction 5

Chapter 1 – Chord-Form Soloing 9

Chapter 2 – Octave-Linking & Long-Form Arpeggios 18

Chapter 3 – Shifting Pentatonic Scales 26

Chapter 4 – Shifting Major & Minor Scales 32

Chapter 5 – Fretboard Geometry 41

About The Author

David Brewster is an honors graduate of the Atlanta Institute of Music and has written several instructional books for Centerstream, Hal Leonard, and Cherry Lane. He also writes articles and lessons for Guitar Player and Premier Guitar magazine. In addition to his publishing background, he's also taught thousands of music students for the School Of Rock, Guitar Center Studios, Ivy Tech Community College, and the National Guitar Workshop (NGW).

He's currently endorsed by Seymour Duncan, DR Strings, Hawk Picks, Hamilton Stands, and Graph Tech. For more information, visit David's website at www.davidbrewstermusic.com

Introduction

Have you ever watched a guitarist move around the fretboard and wonder how they knew where their fingers were going? This is especially true watching a virtuoso-level player perform, as they might move around the neck using abrupt position shifts and effortlessly combine different positions of the fretboard in an instant.

As you watch a knowledgeable player perform these frethand movements, it may seem like an elaborate trick or flashy showmanship, but there are a number of methods to unlock the guitar fretboard that allow players to perform these feats of magic. This book reveals these methods and places these expansive fretboard visualization concepts directly under your fingers, in your mind, and into your playing.

Thanks to the alignment of the frets and strings, which create a "boxed" fretboard visual on the neck, you should begin noticing fingering patterns and fretboard shapes appearing under your fingers and in your mind. Eventually, you'll see how these fingerings are arranged and how you can connect them to assist with moving around the fretboard. It will take practice before you'll be able to use these movements and connections effortlessly, but in time, you'll be able to recreate these ideas with authority and conviction.

This method is arranged into chapters relating to the specific fingering or shape that we'll be targeting and moving around the neck. These will range from basic chord/arpeggio fingerings and partial scale shapes, to extended scale and arpeggio fingerings that will transcend all over the fretboard. As you'll discover, we're going to begin with a handful of basic fingering shapes and expand these ideas into performance ready musical phrases and licks.

One of the most important things to remember with this method is to keep your mind (and ears) open to new fingerings, movements, sounds, and ideas. Several of the ideas shared in this book were borrowed directly from the masters and reveal the origin behind some of the most popular shifted phrases and licks found in rock, blues, and jazz music. In time, you'll be able to construct your own ideas and begin moving around the fretboard with complete confidence, awareness, and control.

A Brief History of Shape Shifting in Music

Historically, there are countless guitarists known for utilizing shape-based ideas in their music and each of these legendary players (along with countless followers) have written and recorded music that skillfully utilize chordal, scalar, and arpeggio-based fingering shapes. These fingerings can be relocated and performed all over the fretboard by incorporating different strings and positions on the neck.

These pioneering frethand movements influenced generations of guitarists all over the world. From monumental recordings and music such as Django Reinhardt's 'Minor Swing' and B.B. King's 'The Thrill Is Gone,' to Van Halen's 'Panama' and Guns And Roses 'Sweet Child O' Mine.' You'll discover shifted fingering fretboard concepts performed (nearly) every time you hear a guitarist play a riff, fill, solo, or melodic phrase in music.

One of the main reasons guitarists base the bulk of their ideas around fingering shapes, fretboard patterns, and visual movements on the neck, relates to the overall layout and design of the instrument. Since you're in constant view of your fingers, strings, and fretboard while playing, you can't help but to begin visualizing the various patterns, shapes, and fretboard fingerings that appear before your eyes.

For many players, these fingering patterns and shapes are recalled by visualizing the finger movement of what they see on the neck while playing a lick, phrase, or idea. Eventually the fingering becomes a simplified way of remembering how to perform a specific section of music. With this in mind, there are plenty of guitarists that don't visualize fingering shapes and fretboard patterns while playing, but you'll find a number of musicians admitting that many of the things they perform are based around simple fingering concepts, shapes, and frethand movements.

Gypsy-jazz guitar legend Django Reinhardt

Selecting a fingering shape and moving it around the fretboard is a simple concept, yet a wealth of melodies, phrases, and licks can be created by using this approach. If you trace this shape-based playing back to the original sources, you'll uncover a stash of licks, phrases, and discoveries generated by the early pioneers and giants of the guitar. This includes early guitar legends such as Django Reinhardt, Charlie Christian, Wes Montgomery, and B.B. King. Each of these guitar greats (and many others) are responsible for the general fretboard approach and shape-based direction that guitarists have maintained all of these decades later.

Blues guitar legend B.B. King

Many of the approaches uncovered by these pioneering musicians created a melodic blueprint for many to follow in their footsteps and paved the way for future generations. Their musical experimentation, innovation, and guidance shaped the overall style, sound, and performance approach that guitarists have continued to use to this day.

One of the most important names in blues music was the legendary icon B.B. King, and while the lengthy list of music and recordings associated with his career is beyond impressive, King has a famous scale shape named after him, known as the "B.B. King box." This familiar and expressive melodic fingering shape can be moved around the fretboard and played in various keys, which King skillfully used during his entire career and influenced millions of guitarists and musicians in the process.

Another famous blues musician named Albert King influenced generations of players, including several important blues and rock players, such as Jimi Hendrix and Stevie Ray Vaughan. Albert has his own scale shape (or "box") named after him, which has been passed around and used by every blues and rock guitarist worth mentioning. Albert's signature scale fingering (or "box") is based around the minor pentatonic scale and features a nuts-and-bolts fingering that can be moved around the neck to access various keys and playing positions.

Through studying classic blues and rock music, you'll find plenty of guitarists borrowing these shapes and exploratory fingering movements. This includes the previously mentioned guitar legend Jimi Hendrix, who directly borrowed various ideas from blues guitar legends to build his own style and sound, which pushed his music and guitar playing to even greater heights.

To hear this blues-influenced spark of creativity, listen to classic Hendrix songs such as 'Purple Haze' and 'Manic Depression,' which inspired a new generation of guitarist. Hendrix's musical and stylistic influence can distinctly be heard in the music that was created and released during his short career, and he single-handedly redefined what the electric guitar was capable of musically, by shaping a new direction for rock and blues guitarists to explore in the future.

Guitarists continued to borrow the pioneering ideas discovered and crafted by the pioneers of the instrument and mutated these approaches to create the new sounds and styles, which exploded throughout the 1960's and 1970's. Tracing the origin of specific guitar licks and phrases to the original source will expose these borrowed ideas, and this recycling of ideas can create new music and develop individual playing styles.

Psychedelic rock guitar legend Jimi Hendrix

One of the greatest electric guitarists to emerge during this discovery period is Eddie Van Halen, who's adept at shaping great tone and popularized several playing techniques that guitarists immediately began to explore. Van Halen has a knack for taking simple ideas and reworking them in fresh and exciting ways. Eddie's sonic output is adored by millions of players all over the world, while his unique approach to playing the guitar and creating music paved the way for the variety of music that flourished during the 1980's and beyond.

Rock guitar legend Eddie Van Halen

Many of the ideas Van Halen popularized and explored were similar (or related) to his peers, but it was the way he combined everything that helped separate him from other players and helped pave the way for the next generation of virtuoso guitarist. An explosion of hyperactive shred guitar playing occurred around this time, and simultaneously changed how guitarists in the rock and metal world played and approached their instrument.

While sifting through the mountain of guitar music created during the 1980's and 1990's, you'll locate plenty of new approaches and further developments of musical ability emanating from the skilled guitarists found during this period. From shred masters such as Yngwie Malmsteen, Steve Vai, and Paul Gilbert, to classic rock and blues giants like Gary Moore, Warren Haynes, and Joe Bonamassa. Collectively, these players discovered new approaches to playing the guitar and the creation of bold music in a rock, metal, and blues style. Legendary jazz and fusion players moved onward during this time as well, as inspired jazz-fusion music coming from John Scofield, Pat Metheny, Scott Henderson, and Mike Stern can be located and analyzed.

Shred guitar legend Steve Vai

By continuing to follow these concepts and ideas into the modern age, you'll distinctly hear these music-making methods continuing to flourish and evolve in today's music, with modern masters such as Guthrie Govan, Tosin Abasi, Jeff Loomis, and Mark Lettieri leading the way.

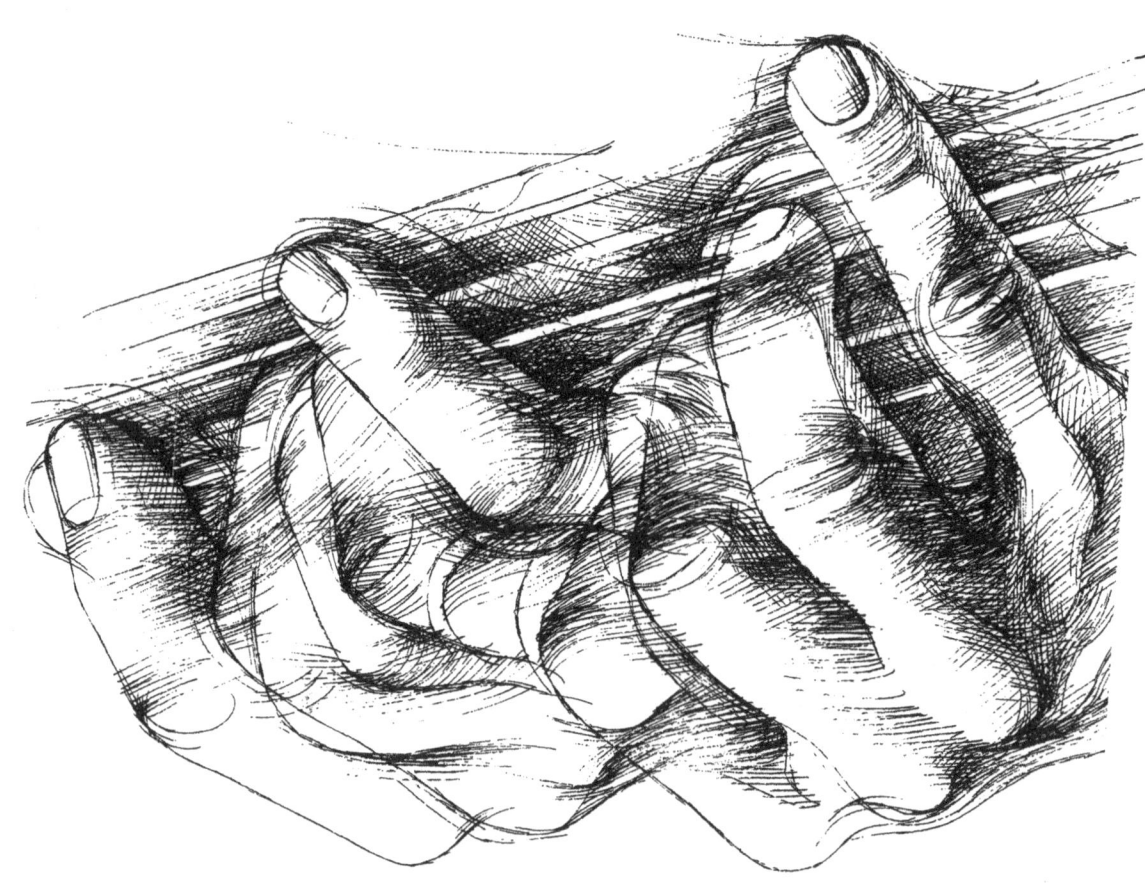

Chapter 1 – *Chord-Form Soloing*

The first chapter explores a popular concept of adapting the fingering shapes we normally relate to strummed chords or rhythm-based playing into single-note melodies, licks, and phrases. The concept we're flirting with here is known as *chord-form soloing* and involves targeting the fingering shape of a chord using a single-note melodic approach. Chord-form soloing is very common in a variety of music and is clearly documented in the style of legends such as Jimi Hendrix, Jimmy Page, David Gilmour, Eddie Van Halen, Slash, and countless others.

To begin working with this concept, instead of holding your fingers down and allowing the notes of a chord to ring together, the idea here involves fretting and sounding each note separately as they're performed. Think of these fretted chord-clusters as targeted melodic arpeggio fingerings while becoming acquainted with this concept.

To get started, let's take a simple D major chord fingering located in open-position and modify the overall function for this group of fretted notes. Instead of strumming or arpeggiating this chord using a rhythm-based approach, take this fingering and create something melodic and musical. Play through **Ex.1** to get things rolling, featuring a basic D major chord fingering in open-position and played melodically (one-note-at-a-time).

Ex.1 – D Major Arpeggio Fingering

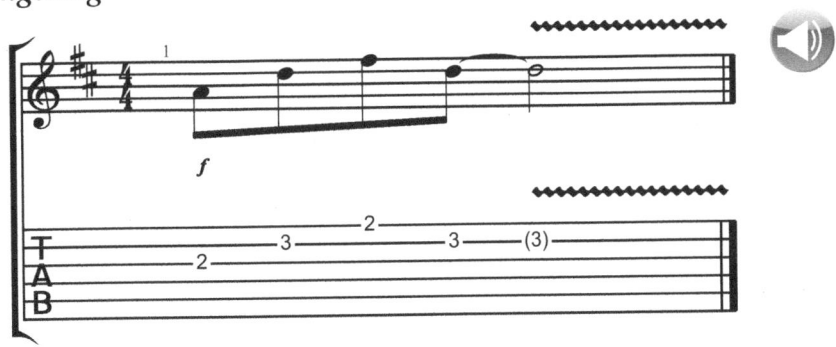

Be sure that you're playing this combination of fretted notes in a singular melodic fashion, instead of strumming or plucking through this as a traditional ringing chord. Remember, we're searching for new melodic possibilities using this chord-based concept, so keep this basic approach in mind as you move forward.

Once you've performed this three-note fingering melodically, you should expand the range of notes we're using on the neck by locating the G triad fingering found at the seventh fret and the A triad fingering found at the ninth fret. These additional positions reveal expanded areas that you can target and solo from, which will align your fingers to discover additional melodic phrases, movements, and possibilities as you move forward. This trio of arpeggio fingerings outlines a common D-G-A chord progression and focuses around an ultra-popular I-IV-V chord progression in the key of D major.

Ex.2 locates these shifted D-G-A arpeggio variations and be sure to memorize the positions on the neck you're visiting as you move through this example. Fretboard visualization concepts will help you recall various fingerings and frethand movements in the future.

Ex.2 – D-G-A Melodic Fingerings

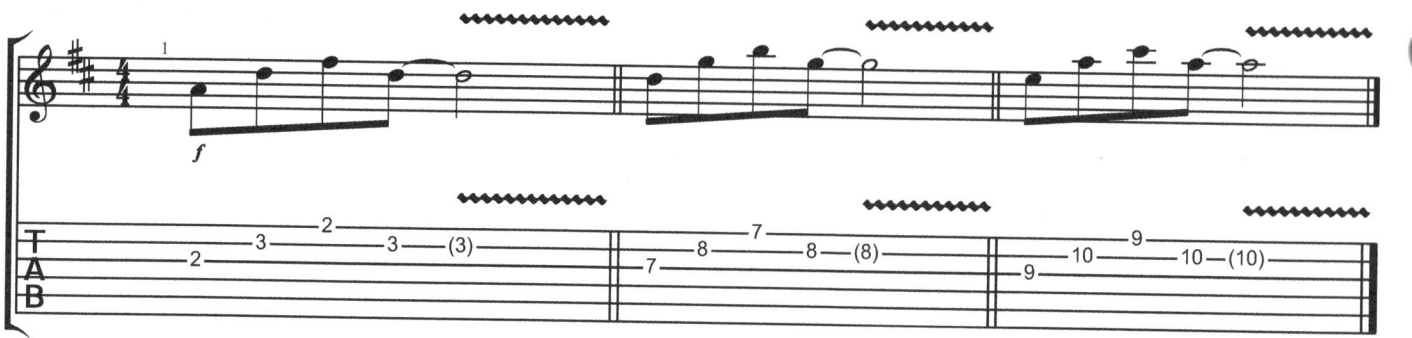

The fretboard diagram in *Fig.1* reveals a birds-eye view behind the physical relocation of this arpeggio fingering to other locations on the neck. This visual guide should open a few things in your mind as you begin playing and experimenting with this shifted-fingering concept.

[*Fig.1* – D-G-A Major Arpeggio Fingerings]

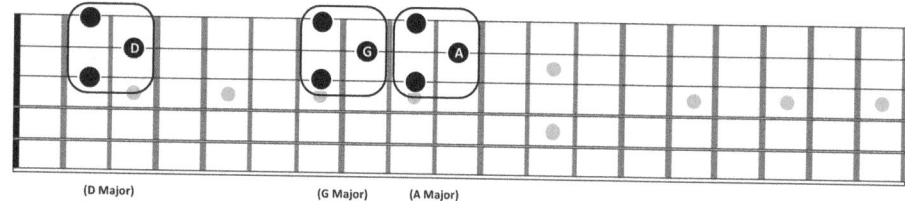

To expand upon the arpeggio we've targeted, **Ex.3** adds a new note to the mix - the note G combined with the D major triad. This modification is common and creates a Dsus4 tonality, but we're searching for new melodic possibilities using this fretboard fingering, so the additional G note functions as a passing tone by blending-in with the original triad during this expanded idea.

Ex.3 – Dsus4 Melodic Targeting

Now that we've added the note G to a D major arpeggio, we can relocate this new sequence of notes to higher positions by apply it to the G and A major arpeggios. This fretboard expansion will help you variate the sound of these three melodic shapes and shifts this musical concept around the fretboard.

Ex.4 will help you see how to move these modified chord clusters around the neck and outline the I-IV-V progression at the same time. This example thoroughly reveals the approach of targeting and mapping the fretboard using this expanded fingering concept as a guide.

Ex.4 – *Dsus4-Gsus4-Asus4 Melodic Phrases*

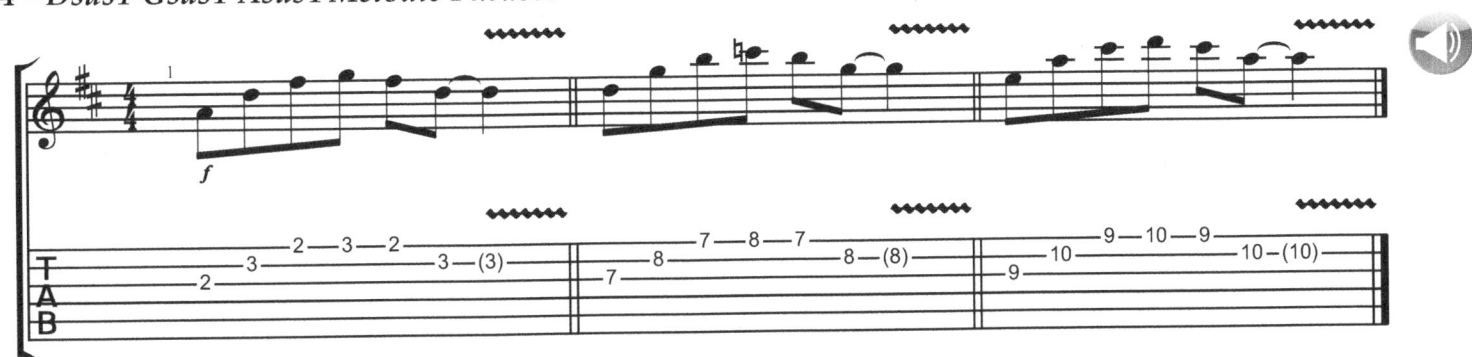

Once you've practiced these fingerings melodically over the D-G-A progression, you should locate additional ways of expanding this idea on the neck. **Ex.5** introduces adding the note A on the fifth fret of the high E string, which is an octave higher than the A found at the beginning of this example. This additional note will allow new melodic phrases and licks to develop, which will greatly expand the usefulness for this trio of melodic arpeggio fingerings.

Ex.5 – *Expanded Melodic Fingerings (D-G-A)*

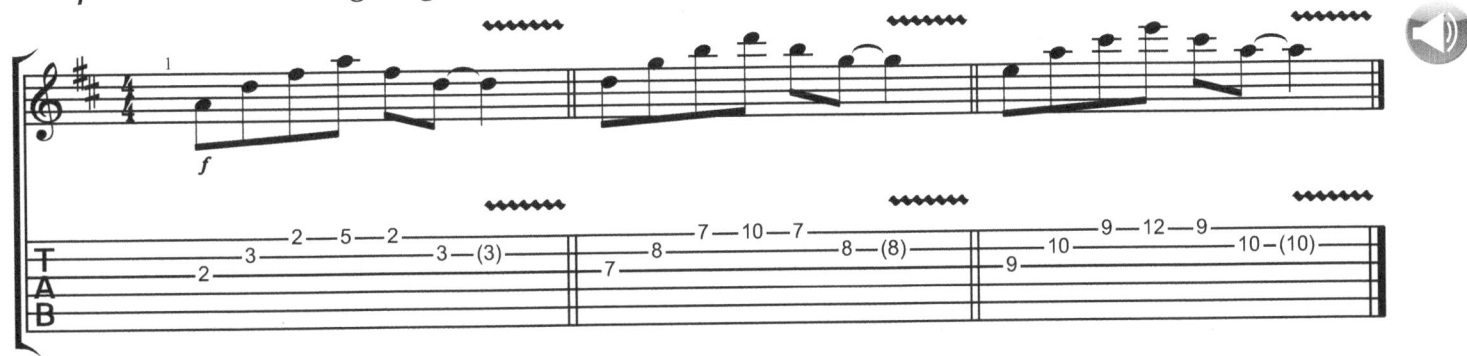

Once you're comfortable with the previous example, you should practice different combinations of melodic movement and targeted notes, using the D-G-A chord progression as a starting point. As you can see, **Ex.6** takes this melodic concept to a new level by applying a melodic legato motif to the three-chord progression.

Ex.6 – *Combination Phrases (D/Dsus4-G/Gsus4-A/Asus4)*

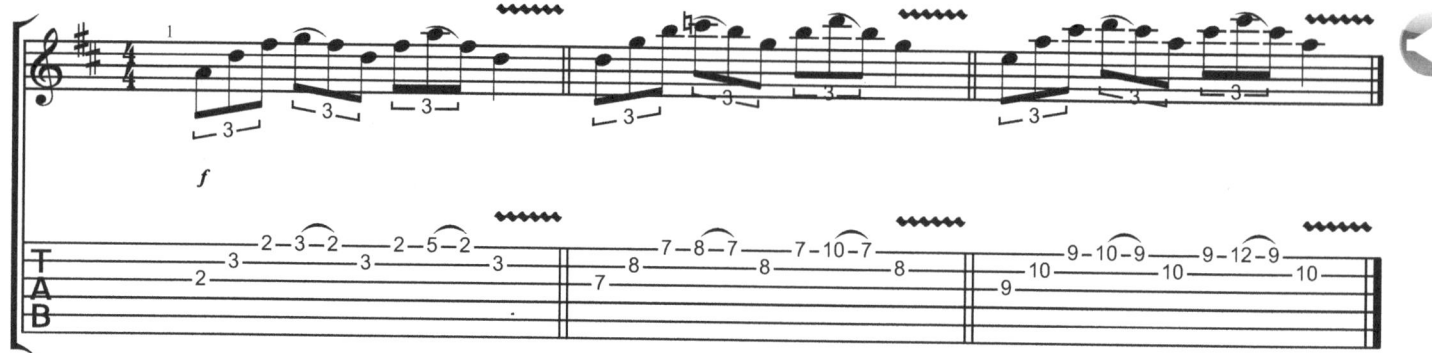

To give this arpeggio fingering a solid finish, practice the next example, which is reminiscent to the melodic motif from The Allman Brothers classic instrumental 'Jessica.' **Ex.7** features a variation of this famous melody and shifts the fingering through a rearranged A-G-D chord progression, which is the same progression we were previously using, but in reverse order.

Ex.7 – *A-G-D Melodic Phrases*

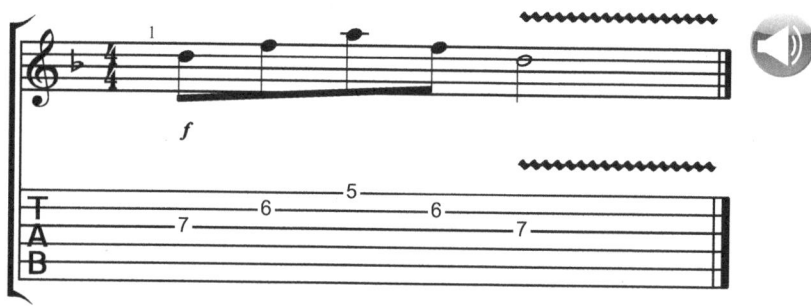

If you keep an ear out for these sounds you'll easily locate this type of arpeggio playing in classic songs, such as 'Runnin' With The Devil' by Van Halen, 'Mother' from Pink Floyd, and 'Sweet Child O' Mine' by Guns And Roses.

The next area we'll explore expands the previous concept further, as the next section introduces a new chord type to the mix and produces an entirely new flavor and tonality. **Ex.8** unveils a three-note D minor triad in the fifth position. This three-note arpeggio falls comfortably under the fingers and provides a very common fingering to utilize and explore in a minor key.

Ex.8 – D Minor Arpeggio Fingering

Once you have a grip using the reworked fingering and minor-key tonality, move this fingering through the I-IV-V chord progression we previously explored, but alter the arpeggio types to reflect a minor key. **Ex.9** demonstrates how to relocate this three-note fingering to create the Dm-Gm-Am arpeggio progression.

Ex.9 – D Minor-G Minor-A Minor Melodic Fingerings

Be sure to study *Fig.2*, which reveals the targeted areas of the fretboard we're exploring in this minor arpeggio-based fingering shift.

[*Fig.2* – D-G-A Minor Arpeggio Fingerings]

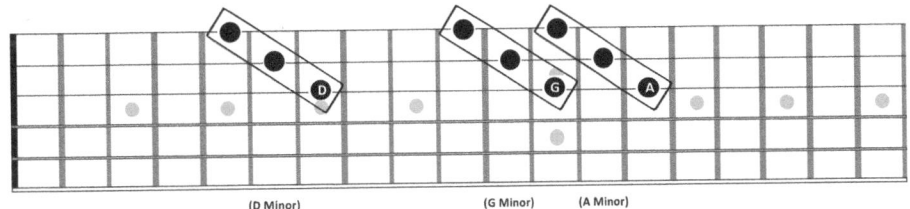

Notably, Eric Clapton used this arpeggio fingering to construct the influential 'All Your Love' solo from his Bluesbreaker days in the 1960's. **Ex.10** features a variation of this famous solo and outlines the Dm-Gm-Am chord progression to create a new melodic idea.

Ex.10 – *Dm-Gm-Am Melodic Phrases*

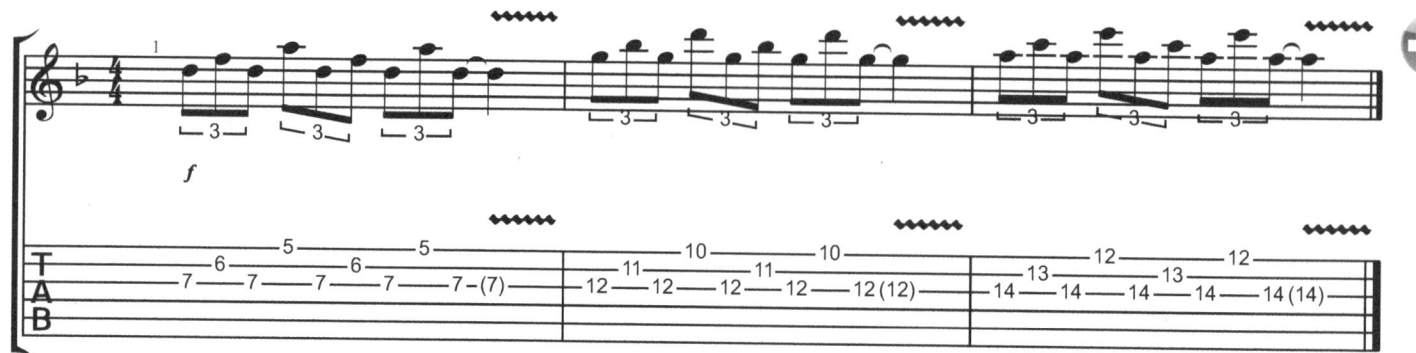

After you've worked through the position shifts in the previous example, you can easily modify and expand the sound of this fingering shape by altering the three-note fingering into a four-note minor seventh tonality. **Ex.11** demonstrates how to approach adding the b7 (the note C) to these three-note shapes and expand the sound to include four-note minor seventh fingerings.

Ex.11 – *Dm7-Gm7-Am7 Melodic Fingerings*

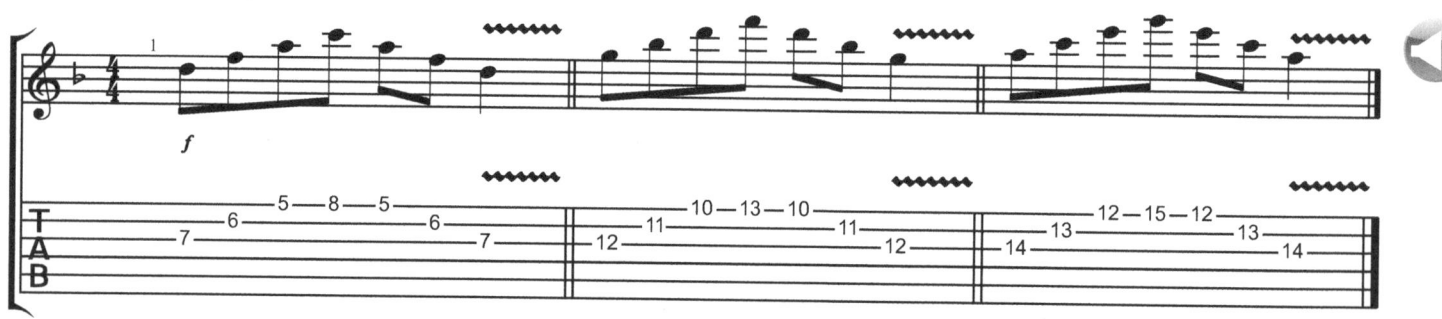

x

As you become comfortable making these alterations and adding additional notes to this arpeggio, you can expand the range of notes we're using to include a lower octave of the b7 to the fingering. Play through **Ex.12** to get a feel and an earful of this useful melodic expansion, which is being used as a passing tone for each arpeggio targeted in this example.

Ex.12 – *Dm7-Gm7-Am7 Melodic Phrases*

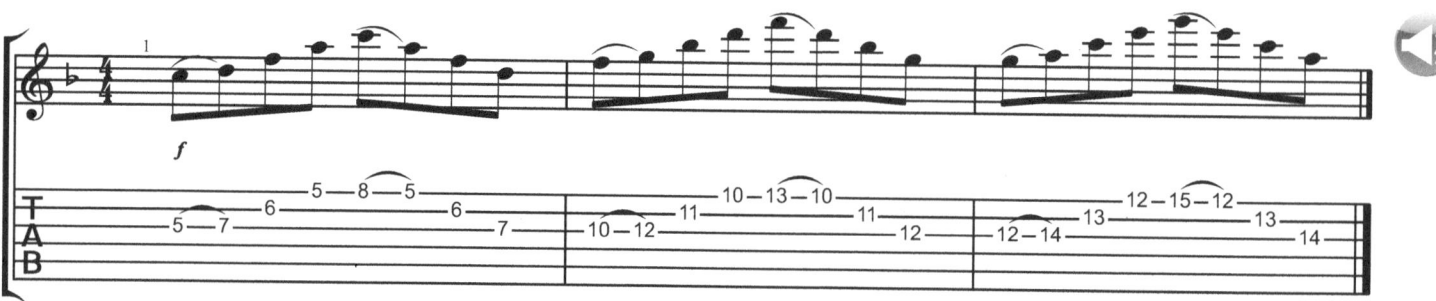

Once you're comfortable playing this expanded fingering in the key of D minor, experiment with moving this fingering to a new grouping of strings, to aid in exploring new keys, tonalities, and melodic ideas. By recycling the three-note fingering we've previously explored and relocating it to the D, G, and B strings, you'll uncover the A major arpeggio fingering demonstrated in **Ex.13**.

Ex.13 – *A Major Arpeggio Fingering*

You can move this fingering to other fretboard locations and mimic previous fretboard shifting movements, but the new grouping of strings we're using will reveal A major, D major, and E major respectively, which is a common I-IV-V progression in the key of A major. To help you visualize this fingering shift on the fretboard, *Fig.3* should make everything easier to see and connect on the neck.

[*Fig.3*]

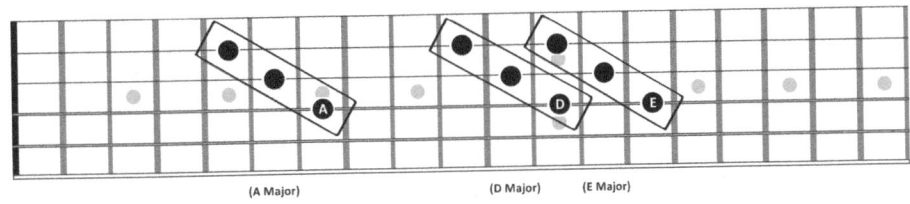

Play through **Ex.14** to get a sample of using this new fingering arrangement and the strong major key tonality we've targeted and uncovered.

Ex.14 – *A-D-E Melodic Fingerings*

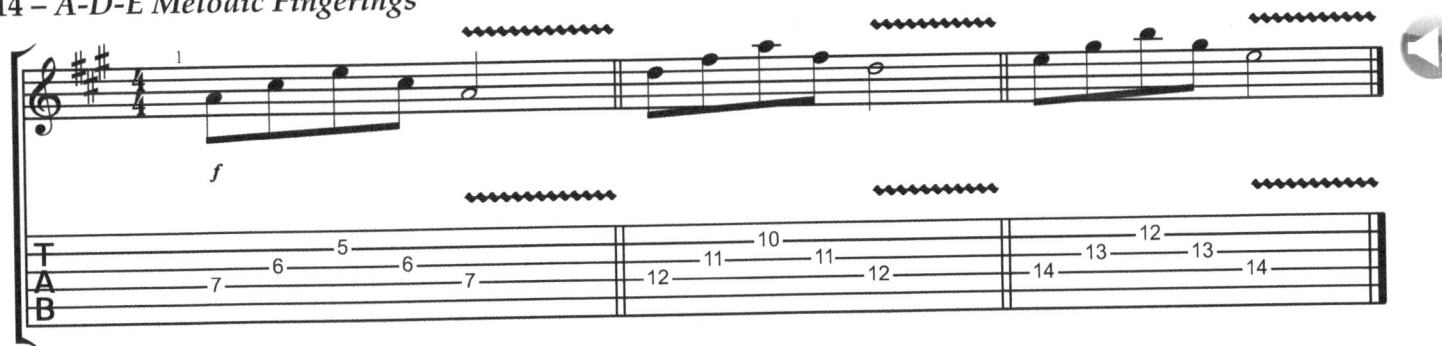

By adding the b7 (G) to the arrangement of notes and fingerings we're playing, you'll unlock a strong bluesy flavor by tapping into the sound of the popular Mixolydian scale, which is one of the modes from the major scale. Be sure to give **Ex.15** some exploratory practice and notice how this new fingering and tonality moves things into bluesier territory.

Ex.15 – *A7-D7-E7 Melodic Phrases*

The next step of expanding this idea includes adding a popular performance technique to the mix. **Ex.16** introduces the concept of adding string-bending to this idea, which will greatly expand the sound of this phrase and successfully moves this concept toward a realistic and musical direction.

Ex.16 – *A7-D7-E7 Melodic Phrases (w/ string-bending)*

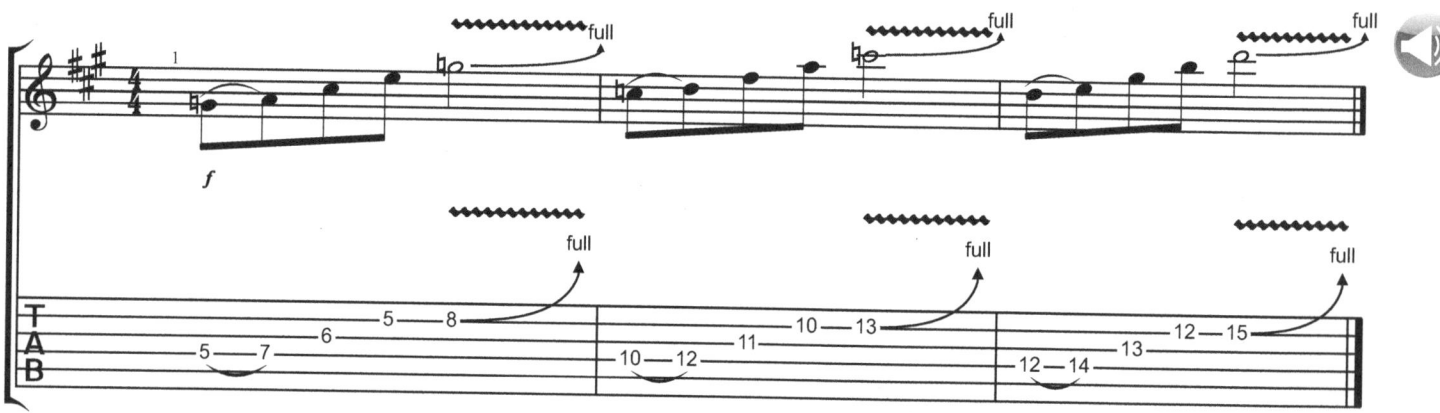

Now that you've experienced how to select a fingering shape and relocate it to another string group, let's rearrange a chord fingering we've previously used and see what new sounds we can discover and unlock. **Ex.17** recycles the fretboard fingering of the D major arpeggio shape from Ex.1, but this variation shifts the fingering over to the D, G, and B strings and creates a useful A7-based arpeggio fingering in the process.

Ex.17 – *A7 Fingering*

To help you visualize what we've relocated and modified on the neck, *Fig.4* features a visual overview to see how and where we've relocated the arpeggio fingering we've selected in Ex.17.

[Fig.4 – A7-D7-E7 Arpeggio Fingerings]

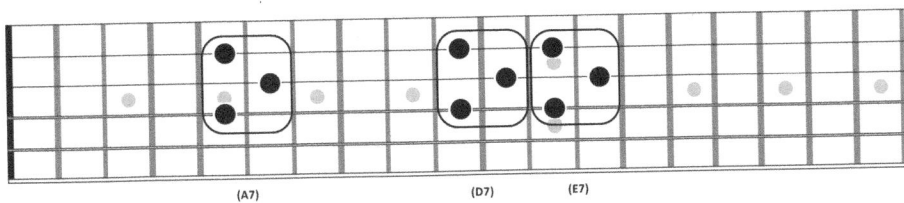

Once you have this arpeggio relocation under your fingers, you should move these melodic fingerings to other fretboard locations and expand this idea further. **Ex.18** continues the exploration of this concept and how you could include the root notes into the phrases, while also shifting it up the fretboard.

Ex.18 – A7-D7-E7 Melodic Fingerings

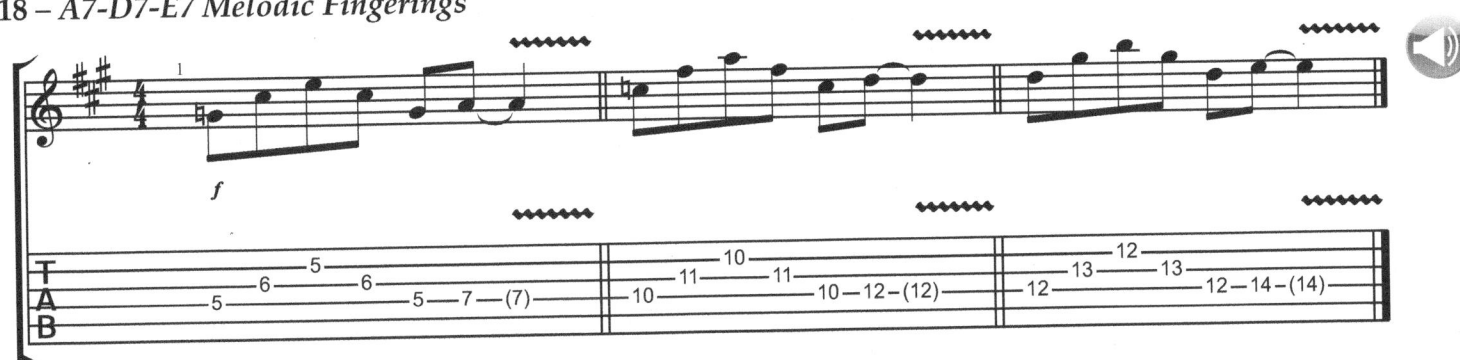

The final example in this chapter expands this concept further, by including legato phrasing to the arpeggio fingerings as they ascend up the fretboard. You can use **Ex.19** as a springboard to help unlock useful blues and rock licks by using this shifted three-note targeted fingering concept as a guide.

Ex.19 – A7-D7-E7 Melodic Phrases

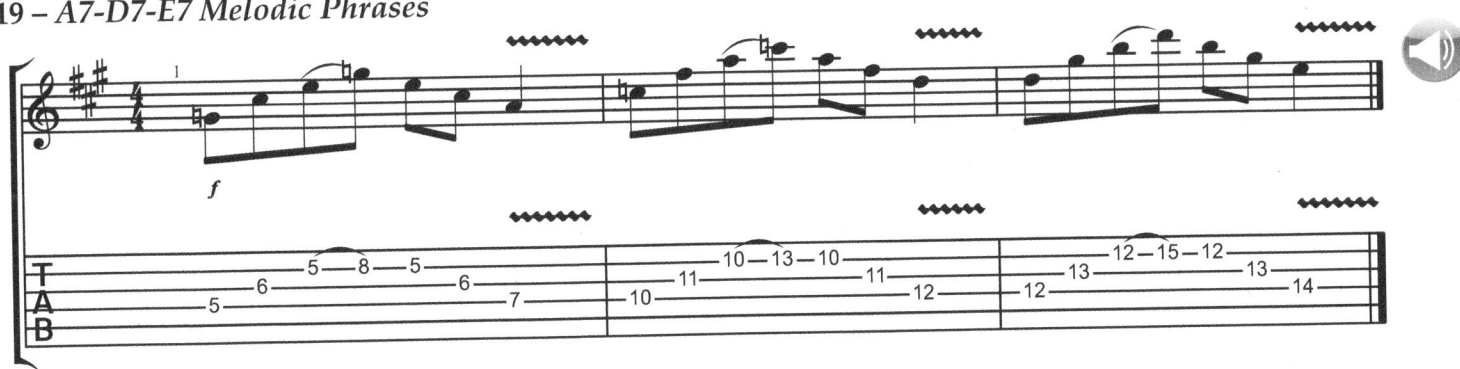

Chapter 2 – Octave Linking & Long-Form Arpeggios

The next chapter involves connecting and combining fretboard areas using octaves around the neck. An *octave* in music is a note separated by twelve half-steps and feature the same note name, but they're noticeably different pitches. Octaves are extremely common in every style of music, including rock, jazz, blues, classical, and country music.

While an octave includes two of the same note names, don't confuse an octave with a unison. A *unison* features two notes that are the exact same pitch and have the same note name, while an octave features two-notes spaced twelve half-steps apart and are noticeably different pitches (low-to-high).

As you begin linking the fretboard using octaves, study **Ex.20** and *Fig.5* carefully, as they display the arrangement of 'B' octaves starting on the low E string (7th fret), to the D string (9th fret), before finally reaching to the 12th fret of the B string at the end. Study this example and diagram carefully and notice the arrangement of octaves forming as you move across the strings and up the fretboard. The importance of understanding this connection of notes along the fretboard will help you combine different areas of the neck.

Ex.20 – B Octaves Mapped

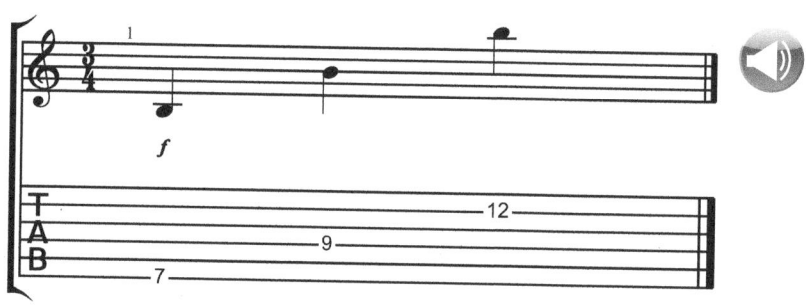

[*Fig.5* – B Octaves "Mapped"]

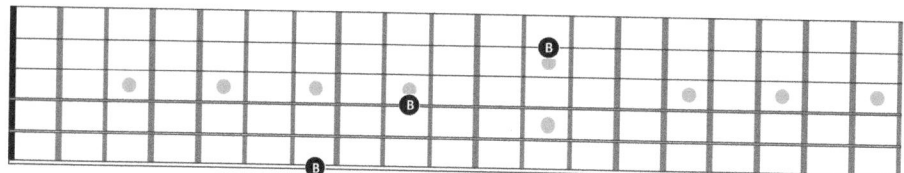

Once you're able to identify and connect these octaves in the key of B, you can begin locating other keys and octaves all over the neck. Doing this type of octave visualization and note identification on the fretboard will greatly increase your awareness of how the notes (and octaves) are arranged and connected all over the neck of the guitar.

Moving forward, the next example begins with the B octaves from the previous example, but adds the minor third (D) to each of these targeted locations. This two-note grouping (B-D) will help you visualize and connect the neck, while simultaneously creating a minor tonality in the process. Play through **Ex.21** to get a feel for this octave-linked two-note concept and notice how it connects along the fretboard.

Ex.21 – *B-D Octave-Linking*

If we add the note F# to this idea, we'll construct a B minor arpeggio (B-D-F#), which will further expand the sound and application of this concept. This expansion into arpeggios will also unravel more of the mystery surrounding the layout of notes on the fretboard. Play through **Ex.22** to get a feel for combining this three-note cluster of notes together, which will give you a visual of how you can move around and connect additional areas of the fretboard.

Ex.22 – *B Minor Arpeggio Octave-Linked*

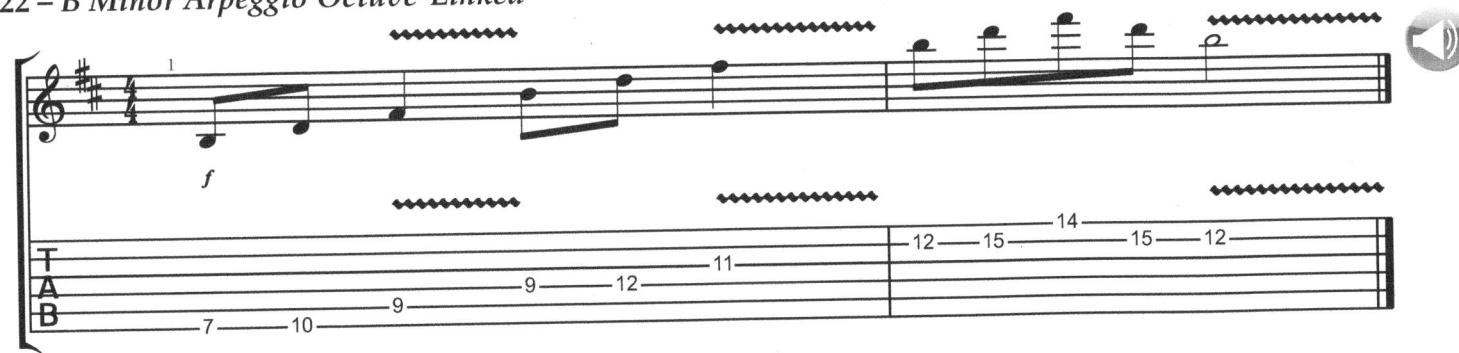

Long-Form Arpeggios

The next area of fretboard discovery adds the b7th (A) to the mix. The additional note added to this fingering changes what we're playing toward traditional four-note arpeggios. These four-note arpeggio fingerings are sometimes called *long-form arpeggios* and produce finger-friendly arpeggio shapes that provide an easy way of looking at the neck and connecting the fretboard.

Playing through **Ex.23** will supply your fingers with a four-note Bm7 arpeggio (B-D-F#-A), which is rather simple to perform and shift around the neck. As you play with this fingering, notice how this four-note fingering connects and relocates around the fretboard.

Ex.23 – B Minor 7 Long-Form Arpeggio

Fig.6 provides a clear view of the fingering and movement we're exploring in the previous example using this Bm7 long-form arpeggio.

[Fig.6 – Bm7 Long-Form Arpeggio Fingering]

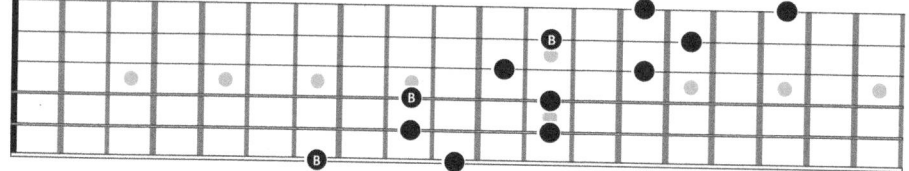

Once this concept is comfortable under your fingers, you can shift this idea to a new key while remaining in the same fretboard position. **Ex.24** and *Fig.7* move this idea to Em7, which is rather easy to visualize thanks to the layout of the fretboard and how octaves connect on the neck. The shift to E minor is created by rearranging the fingering we were previously using for Bm7 and aligning it to match Em7 in this position.

Ex.24 – *E Minor 7 Long-Form Arpeggio*

[*Fig.7 – Em7 Long-Form Arpeggio Fingering*]

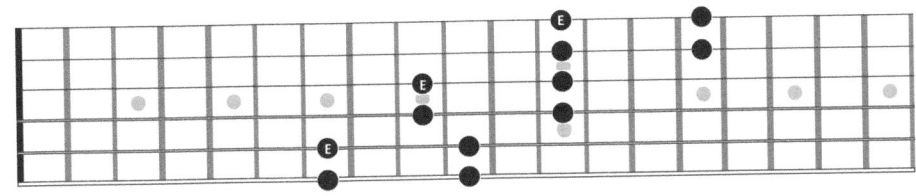

These long-form arpeggio fingerings are useful for exploring additional keys, chord types, and areas on the fretboard. As you move onward with this expansion of the neck and arpeggio-based discovery, be sure to keep an eye out for the shifting movements and general variances with this idea as it moves forward.

Ex.25 reveals the popular E dominant seventh arpeggio, which would sound great over blues and rock-based chord progressions and music.

Ex.25 – *E Dominant 7 Long-Form Arpeggio*

To get a better view of the fingering for the dominant seventh long-form arpeggio, *Fig.8* should help you clearly visualize everything that has changed with this new fingering.

[*Fig.8 – E7 Long-Form Arpeggio Fingering*]

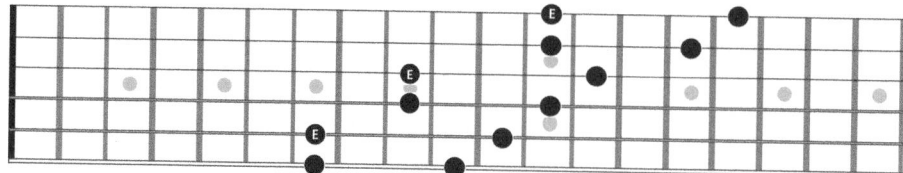

The next arpeggio type to discover includes major seventh arpeggios, as **Ex.26** and *Fig.9* share the next evolution of expanding these long-form arpeggio fingerings in a new tonality and melodic direction.

Ex.26 – E Major 7 Long-Form Arpeggio

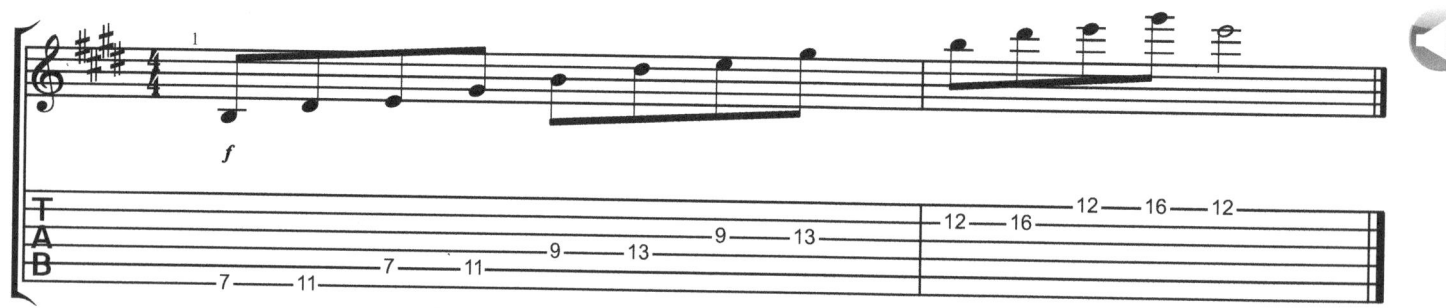

[*Fig.9 – Emaj7 Long-Form Arpeggio Fingering*]

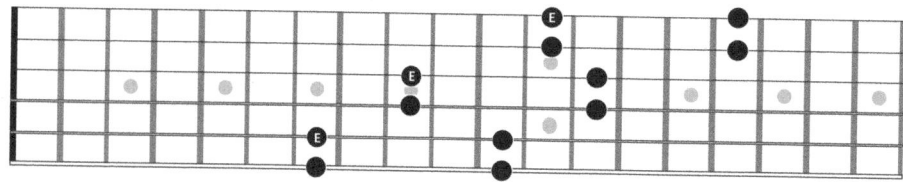

As you move forward with this concept, be sure to visualize and memorize the fretboard diagrams that accompany each of these long-form arpeggio demonstrations. These diagrams will make the process of memorizing these new fingerings and shift-based movements easier now and in the future.

As you can see with the three previous examples, it only takes a little note-alteration and fretboard movement to drastically change the chord type and tonality of what you're playing. As you move forward with this idea, be sure to memorize the specific fingerings and shapes we've explored in this chapter, and attempt moving these ideas to include additional keys, chord types, progressions, and fretboard positions.

To give your fingers and neck awareness a challenge, **Ex.27-29** incorporates the three seventh arpeggios we targeted in the previous section of this chapter, but reverses the direction to create a connected descending variation.

Ex.27 – E Minor 7 Arpeggio (Descending)

Ex.28 - E Dominant 7 Arpeggio (Descending)

Ex.29 – E Major 7 Arpeggio (Descending)

Practicing long-form arpeggios ascending and descending will give your fingers and mind a challenging workout. You may want to practice these arpeggio-based movements as a warm-up exercise around the neck, which will provide a boost for developing additional dexterity and technique in your playing, not to mention the additional benefit of unlocking large sections and areas of the fretboard.

Once you've had an opportunity to practice these long-form arpeggio fingerings, you could combine everything you've learned to create challenging fretboard exercises using this information. **Ex.30** shares an Em7 legato workout to get your fingers fully connected with this position-based movement around the fretboard.

Ex.30 – *Em7 Long-Form Arpeggio Legato Workout*

The ABC's of the Fretboard

The next visualization concept involves a simple idea but creates a challenging note chasing fretboard challenge. The basic premise behind this concept is revealed in **Ex.31**, where we're targeting the first three letters of the alphabet (*A-B-C*) along the neck. This effective fretboard note-visualization exercise reveals and utilizes this three-note grouping everywhere it can be played comfortably on the fretboard.

Ex.31 – *The "ABC's of the Fretboard"*

Once you have a grip using this elementary idea, create some additional musical exercises, licks, phrases, and ideas using this note-targeting exercise. **Ex.32** demonstrates an example of connecting this three-note group using scale-based fingering movements all over the fretboard.

Ex.32 - *"ABC's of the Fretboard" Connected*

To conclude this chapter, you should move this targeted three-note concept to incorporate additional notes and shifting movements to successfully expand this idea all over the neck and reach a variety of keys. As you incorporate additional fingerings, shapes, and movements around the fretboard, notice the various fingering shifts and note groupings that connect the neck. Explore these options and ideas thoroughly by generating some additional melodic licks, phrases, and exercises of your own design.

D'Angelico Deluxe Bedford

Chapter 3 – *Shifting Pentatonic Scales*

For guitarists playing (almost) any musical style, Pentatonic scales have become so common that selecting and incorporating them into this type of practice is beyond logical, especially to assist with unlocking more of the neck using scales and scale-based fingerings.

Historically speaking, one of the earliest influential guitarists known for shifting Pentatonic shapes around the neck is blues music legend Albert King. Albert not only penned a number of important and massively-influential songs, but his expressive and tasteful guitar style directly influenced a number of legendary blues and rock guitarists, including Jimi Hendrix, Stevie Ray Vaughan, Jeff Beck, and Billy Gibbons (to name a few).

To help move things toward Pentatonic-based shifting movements and exploration, **Ex.33** features the common minor Pentatonic "box" scale fingering in F# minor, which is arranged and performed in the second position.

Ex.33 – *F# Minor Pentatonic (Shape 1)*

Ex.34 reveals the second position of the minor Pentatonic scale, adjacent to the "box" fingering in the previous example. If you're unfamiliar with this fingering position, be sure to become acquainted and practice this shape until it feels familiar, as you're going to need skill targeting and using this fingering in the next example.

Ex.34 – *F# Minor Pentatonic (Shape #2)*

Ex.35 features a challenging combination-shift exercise, blending the first and second position of the minor Pentatonic scale into an excellent position-shifting workout. Practice this example slowly until the shifting movements become comfortable, connected, and effortless to perform.

Ex.35 – F# Minor Pentatonic (Shapes 1&2 Connected)

As soon as you're comfortable playing the previous example using an ascending movement, reverse the pattern and begin practicing this idea using a descending movement. **Ex.36** reveals how to perform this tricky fingering maneuver and descending sequence of notes.

Ex.36 – F# Minor Pentatonic (Shapes 1&2 Connected/Descending)

To expand your knowledge and mastery of mixing and shifting Pentatonic scales on the fretboard, the next example features a useful way of combining different positions on the neck. This style of position and shifting has been utilized by guitar greats such as Al Di Meola, Eddie Van Halen, Steve Morse, Eric Johnson, and many other six-string legends.

Ex.37 uncovers how to arrange and ascend the fretboard using two-string note groupings of the minor Pentatonic scale, by maintaining an upward shift movement on the A and low E string. Be sure to practice this example slowly if this style of shifting and movement is uncomfortable or new for you.

Ex.37 – F# Minor Pentatonic on Two Strings (E-A)

Ex.38 features the next string group (A-D) and will help you expand this shifting concept even further.

Ex.38 – F# Minor Pentatonic on Two Strings (A-D)

Ex.39 moves to the next string grouping, by including the D and G strings to this idea. Once again, be sure to practice this example slowly if this fretboard movement and combination of scale positions is new for you.

Ex.39 – F# Minor Pentatonic on Two Strings (D-G)

For the next evolution of this idea, **Ex.40** features the next string group and incorporates the G and B strings while maintaining the position-shifting scale sequencing and movement on the neck.

Ex.40 – F# Minor Pentatonic on Two Strings (G-B)

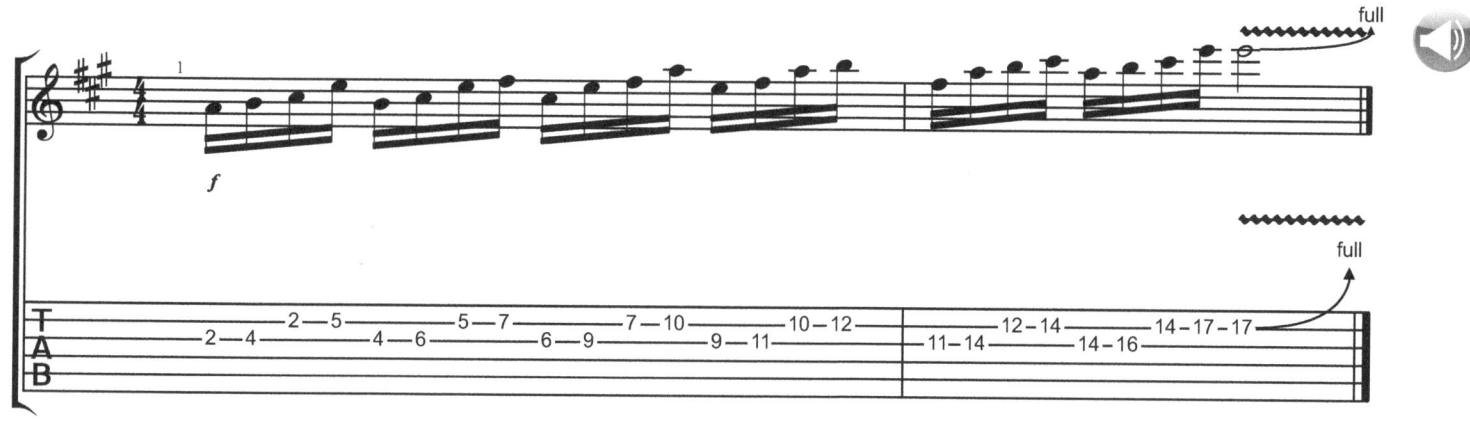

The next example expands this idea to include the B and high E strings, as **Ex.41** provides another useful variation of this interesting Pentatonic-based shifting workout.

Ex.41 – F# Minor Pentatonic on Two Strings (B-E)

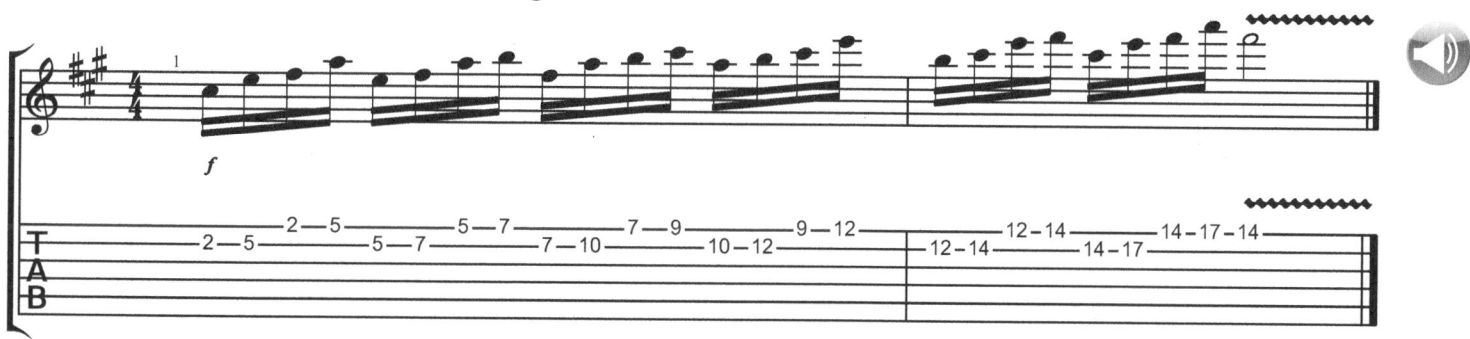

Countless guitarists have shifted Pentatonic scales using an aggressive rock and metal guitar style. This includes players such as Randy Rhoads, "Dimebag" Darrell, Kirk Hammett, and Zakk Wylde. Each of these players (and countless others) have written and recorded hyperactive Pentatonic-based licks and phrases in their music.

Ex.42 shares a descending Zakk Wylde-inspired Pentatonic sequence that he's used for years. Don't be intimidated by a large number of notes or the use of sextuplet rhythms in this example. Begin slow and gradually increase the speed when attempting to perform this hyperactive shifting lick on the neck.

Ex.42 – *Descending Sextuplet Pentatonic Phrase*

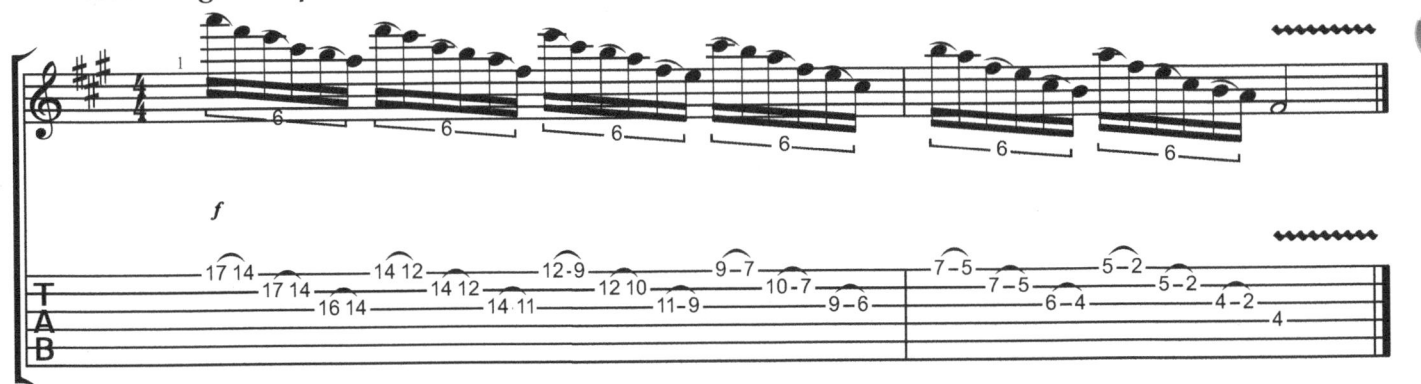

To help move things into a different direction, **Ex.43** introduces the F# Blues scale and morphs these Pentatonic-based ideas into a new tonality and fretboard location.

Ex.43 – *F# Minor Blues Scale*

With this scale successfully under your fingers, attempt to shift it upward on the neck by including and targeting A and C minor Blues scales respectively. **Ex.44** tackles this challenging fretboard shifting workout, but move slowly until you're comfortable with this type of position-shifting and targeted fretboard movement.

Ex.44 – *F#-A-C Minor Blues Scale Workout*

Ex.45 is a descending version of the previous example and begins on the high E instead of the low E string. This variation provides a mirror-image of the previous idea, which makes this example a great shifting/fingering challenge that you can practice and explore. Take your time if this shifting and movement are new for you.

Ex.45 – *F#-A-C Minor Blues Scale Workout (Descending)*

Now that you've learned and performed this collection of Pentatonic-based scale sequences, exercises, and ideas, you should continue with this concept and locate additional exercises and phrases of your own creation. The more you become comfortable moving around the fretboard and combining different scale and fingering shapes together, the better you'll become at recalling this type of movement and information in the future. Eventually, you'll begin moving around the neck and enjoy effortless movement all over the neck.

Chapter 4 – *Shifting Major & Minor Scales*

As your fingers and mind become comfortable moving, shifting, and performing the previous exercises and ideas, you should expand these concepts further and explore full seven-note major and minor scales. Now that you've explored the approach of blending and connecting different scale positions on the neck, you can begin creating and performing expanded licks, phrases, and ideas.

While the previous chapter focused on five-note Pentatonic scales, this chapter will center around seven-note diatonic scales and modes. This scalar expansion requires more thought, planning, and technical focus to perform properly. This is due to the inclusion of two additional notes to the major and minor scale structure. You'll notice many of the fingering combinations and movements we're using are based on three-note per-string fingerings and patterns, instead of the two-note/two-finger Pentatonic-based fingering shapes used in the previous chapter.

The ideas explored in this chapter are based on ideas generated by a group of phenomenal guitarists that have created their own approaches of using and applying this information. A few of these high-octane players include Steve Vai, Joe Satriani, Yngwie Malmsteen, Paul Gilbert, and Eric Johnson. These inspiring guitarists have spent the majority of their careers chasing notes, licks, and phrases all over the fretboard, so you should watch and learn from these masters to discover additional ways of connecting and moving around the guitar neck.

To unlock this method of fingering movement and scale discovery, the next example targets a one-octave A Aeolian scale centered in the fifth position. Aeolian is also known as the natural minor scale, so if you're already familiar with that name, notice that Aeolian is identical to natural minor, but uses the Greek-derived modal name. Play through **Ex.46** to identify and begin using this common scale, which is found in every style of music.

Ex.46 – *A Natural Minor (Aeolian)*

As soon as you have the one-octave fingering of this scale under your fingers, you can expand this fingering using the octave-linking concept we explored in Chapter 2. Playing through **Ex.47** will help you see how to connect the fretboard using this fingering concept, which links shifted octaves up the neck and across the fretboard.

Ex.47 – *A Aeolian (Three Octaves)*

The next method of expanding this concept involves removing the seventh from the scale, revealing a simplified fingering for you to practice and explore. **Ex.48** features the scale from in the previous example with the seventh (G) removed, to create a connected six-note fingering using octaves and moves easily up the neck.

Ex.48 – *A Aeolian (Without the 7th)*

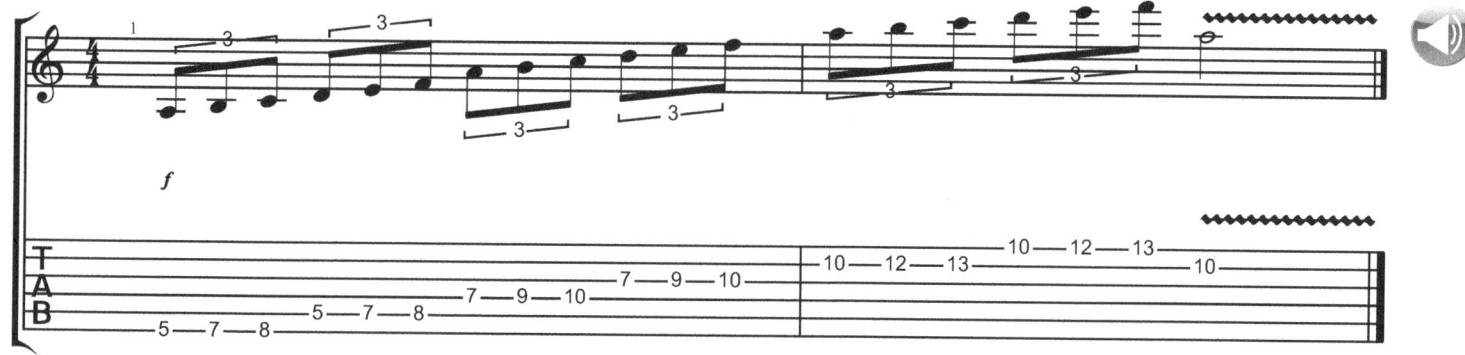

To visualize how the removal of the seventh from this scale creates a noticeable pattern of notes on the fretboard, examine *Fig.10* to see how this scale is arranged in the previous example.

[*Fig.10* – Six-note A Aeolian Fingering]

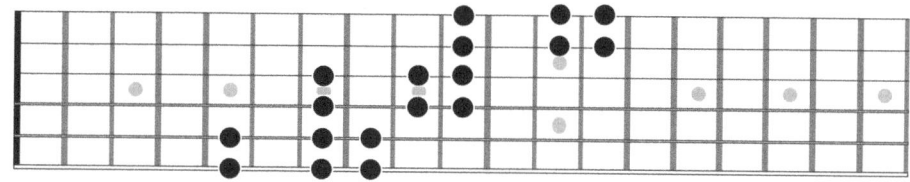

Now you've experienced how this scale can be connected on the neck, you can decide how to reintroduce the note G that was removed in Ex.48. **Ex.49** reveals how you can approach accessing the missing G by incorporating a pinky shift between the notes F and G respectively.

Ex.49 – *A Aeolian (w/ pinky shift-slide)*

After you've included this note using your pinky, you can variate how (and where) you're accessing this note by targeting it using an index finger slide, as **Ex.50** reveals.

Ex.50 – *A Aeolian (w/ index shift-slide)*

Be sure to play between these two approaches of reintroducing G to the scale, and begin creating additional licks, phrases, and exercises that experiment with how to arrange these targeted notes on the fretboard. This type of practice will help you view the neck in a new way and will keep things fresh every time you pick up your guitar and move around the neck.

The next concept involves discovering a better view of the neck, by selecting a single targeted root note and locating the related octaves all over the fretboard. To help you get started with this type of practice and fretboard visualization, **Ex.51** and *Fig.11's* visual guidance locates the note A all over the fretboard. Once you're aware of where this root note is located around the neck, you should memorize this diagram thoroughly to pinpoint and target the location of this selected note everywhere that it can be performed.

Ex.51 – *A Octaves Mapped on the Fretboard*

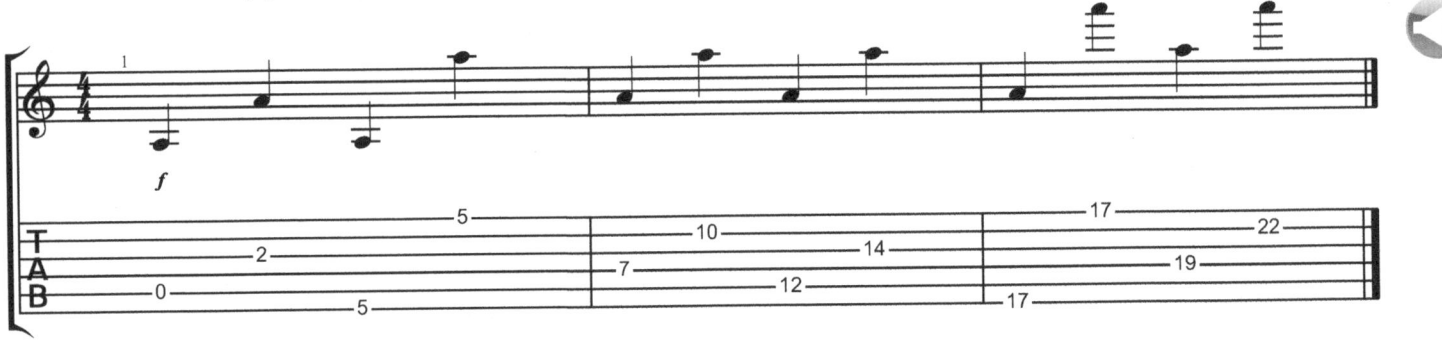

[*Fig.11 – A Octaves Mapped on the Fretboard*]

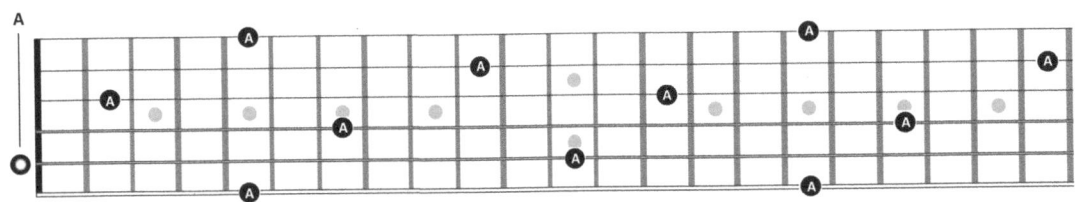

The next example reveals a variation to the one-octave Aeolian shapes from this chapter, which are constructed from the A root-notes that we're targeted all over the neck in Ex.51. As you can see, **Ex.52** targets the most logical locations of performing the one-octave fingering for this scale, by skillfully avoiding any fretboard positions or areas where a full-octave of this scale is unable to accommodate or perform.

Ex.52 – *A Aeolian Mapped & Connected*

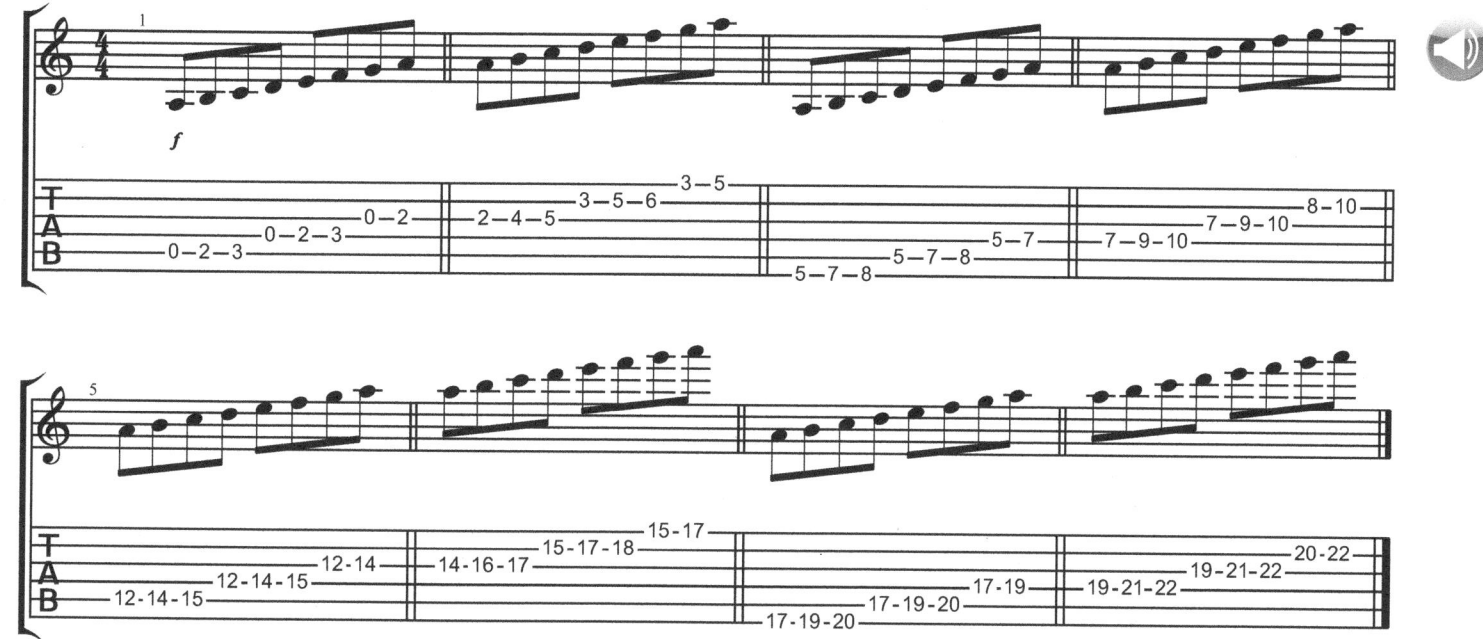

In time, your awareness and understanding of the fretboard will improve significantly and you'll be able to locate notes, scale fragments, arpeggio fragments, and all sorts of melodic information in an instant. The next step of moving this concept forward involves taking these one-octave scale connections and converting the fingerings to include two-octave scale movement around the neck. **Ex.53** will help you locate how you could expand the scale to include more real estate on the fretboard and reach a two-octave scale fingering.

Ex.53 – *A Aeolian Connection #1*

Ex.54 shares the next position of Aeolian in the key of A Minor, revealing how the connection between these octaves connect the fretboard.

Ex.54 – *A Aeolian Connection #2*

As you continue shifting through these connected fingerings and shapes, notice and memorize any fingering patterns or connections that allow these scales to be combined and shifted along the neck. Pay considerable attention to these connections, which will help you remember how to move other scales around the neck in the future.

The next example creates a slight alteration to the Aeolian scale formula, by raising the last note of this scale (the seventh - G) a half-step to G#. This alteration creates the A Harmonic Minor scale, which is a very popular exotic scale found in plenty of rock, jazz, metal, and classical music.

Ex.55 features this popular scale and recycles the fingering from the previous example. Be sure to compare both of the scales side-by-side, which will help you to see what was specifically altered and how to recycle this information in a new direction.

Ex.55 – *A Harmonic Minor Scale Conversion*

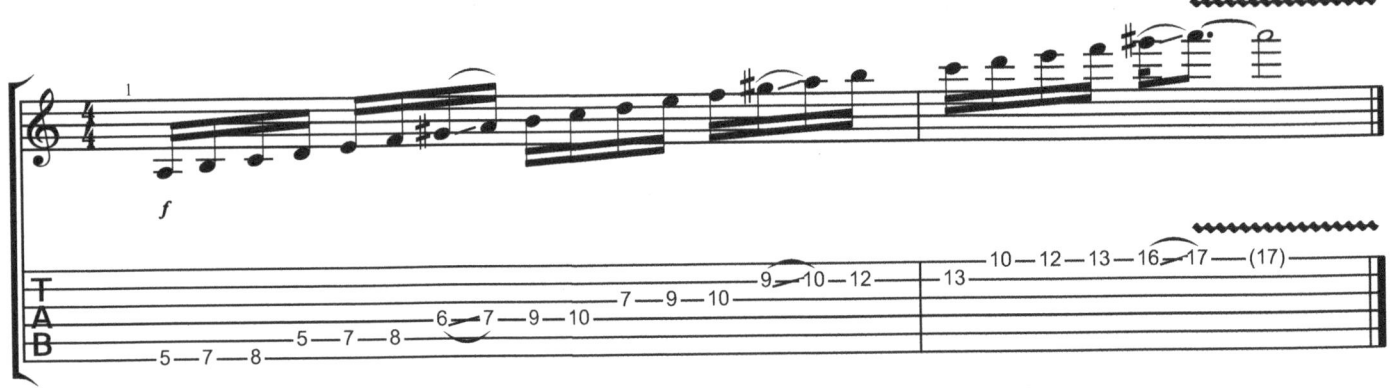

The next area we'll explore involves returning to Aeolian, but aligns the scale to be performed entirely on the low E string. Single-string scales will help you rapidly visualize and unlock the fretboard. This area of study will help you notice the gaps present between the notes of this scale and visualize them directly on the neck. This method of navigating the fretboard also creates an entirely new way of moving around the neck and combining different scale positions together. Play through **Ex.56** to become acquainted with single-string scale performance and note arrangement.

Ex.56 – *A Aeolian on the Low E String*

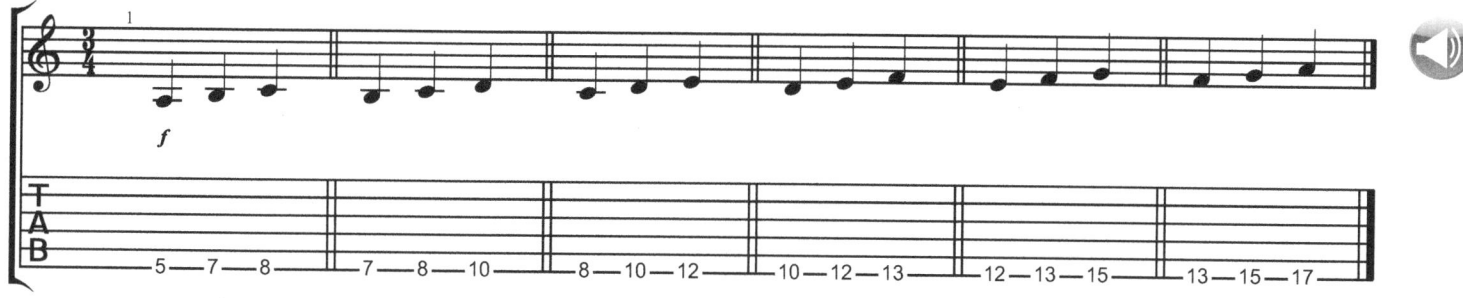

This example showcases how a one-octave scale can be shifted up the fretboard. Notice the three distinct fingerings that appear in this example – which include the *half-step/whole-step* fingering (#1), the *whole-step/half-step* fingering (#2), and the *whole-step/whole-step* fingering (#3). These three fingerings are the most common three-note per-string shapes performed on the guitar and should be practiced thoroughly before moving ahead in this chapter.

The next example targets the three fingering shapes previously shown, but uses them in a different way. This section uncovers the most common fingerings for the seven modes generated from the major scale. If you're unfamiliar with the construction of modal scales and theory, I would highly recommend studying this area of music and possibly attend a music theory class or seminar. Doing this will help you understand what modal scales are and how you can approach using these useful sounds and textures in your music.

Ex.57 features the most common three-note per-string modal fingerings performed on the guitar. Study this example carefully and be sure to notice each of the three general frethand fingerings from the previous example. Take your time with these fingering shapes and fretboard connections and gradually begin including this exercise as part of your daily practice routine.

Ex.57 – *Parallel View of the Modes from the Major Scale (in A)*

To move from the introduction to the deep end using this concept, **Ex.58** introduces A Ionian to the mix and the next area reveals how to perform each of the seven modes using the connected fingerings we've previously uncovered. Ionian is also known as the major scale and as you play through this example, notice how these fingerings are extended to accommodate performing three-octaves on the neck.

Ex.58 – *A Ionian*

Ex.59 features a three-octave fingering of the next mode in the cycle, A Dorian. The Dorian mode is a very popular tonality and can be heard in a variety of rock, jazz, and fusion music, especially the music of six-string Latin-rock legend Carlos Santana.

Ex.59 – *A Dorian*

The next fingering converts the scale into the exotic A Phrygian mode. The Phrygian mode featured in **Ex.60** has an exotic flavor and can be distinctly heard in plenty of rock, metal, jazz, and flamenco music. Richie Blackmore and Yngwie Malmsteen love to utilize this exotic modal scale sound in their music.

Ex.60 – *A Phrygian*

Moving forward, the next example features the interesting and modern sound of the Lydian mode, which can be heard in the music of Frank Zappa, Steve Vai, and John Petrucci, to name a few. **Ex.61** unveils a method of arranging this popular scale using a three-octave fingering.

Ex.61 - *A Lydian*

The bluesy Mixolydian mode is next in the modal scale cycle and **Ex.62** shows how to arrange this popular scale using a connected three-octave form. As you play through this familiar-sounding example, notice the small shifts and fingering alterations occurring as you move from one modal fingering to another. You can hear Mixolydian being used by legends such as Jimmy Page, Jeff Beck, and Slash, in a mountain of classic blues, rock, and funk music.

Ex.62 – *A Mixolydian*

Next up is Aeolian and **Ex.63** reveals how to perform this previously-featured scale using a three-octave fingering and larger segment of the fretboard. There are countless guitar giants known for using Aeolian in their music, including powerhouse metal players such as Randy Rhoads, Kirk Hammett, and "Dimebag" Darrell.

Ex.63 – *A Aeolian*

The final fingering in this chapter features targeting related to the sinister Locrian mode, which has a dark diminished-related tonality and can be found in plenty of music. **Ex.64** shares this final mutation, which will help you become acquainted with the exotic flavor and sound this scale generates. You may recognize this odd tonality being used in the music of artists as diverse as jazz legend John Scofield, avant-garde shred guitarist Buckethead, or metal legends Slayer.

Ex.64 – *A Locrian*

D'Angelico Excel DC

Chapter 5 – *Fretboard Geometry*

The final chapter in this book focuses on uncovering various directional methods that allow you to shift and move around the fretboard in different ways. The use of the word "geometry" in this chapter revolves around the directional terminology we'll be borrowing from basic geometry. As you notice how guitarists move around the neck, you'll discover four main directional movements that can be visualized on the neck while shifting around. These direction-based terms include *vertical*, *horizontal*, *diagonal*, and *reverse-diagonal* movement on the fretboard.

To understand this area of direction-based movement and discovery, **Ex.65** shares a two-octave C# minor Pentatonic scale and fingering, which will be the basis and foundation for the first section of this chapter. As you play through this popular scale and fingering, notice the vertical movement occurring on the fretboard as the notes ascend and move across the strings.

Ex.65 – *C# Minor Pentatonic*

To give this sequence of notes more depth, **Ex.66** and *Fig.12* contain an ascending sequence of notes using a vertical motion across the strings and fretboard.

Ex.66 – *C# Minor Pentatonic (Vertical Movement)*

[*Fig.12 – Vertical Movement*]

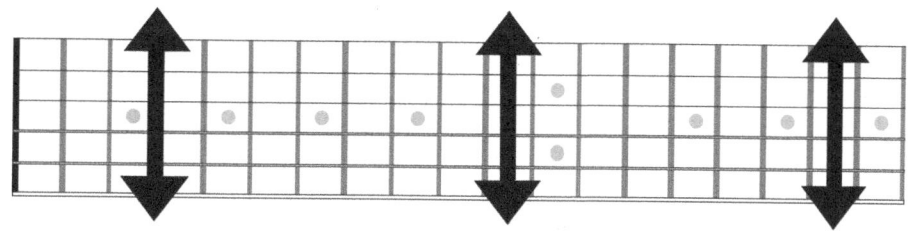

The next type of directional movement across the strings and fretboard is featured in **Ex.67** and *Fig.13*, revealing an ascending horizontal approach that moves along the strings and up the neck.

Ex.67 – *C# Minor Pentatonic (Horizontal Movement)*

[*Fig.13 – Horizontal Movement*]

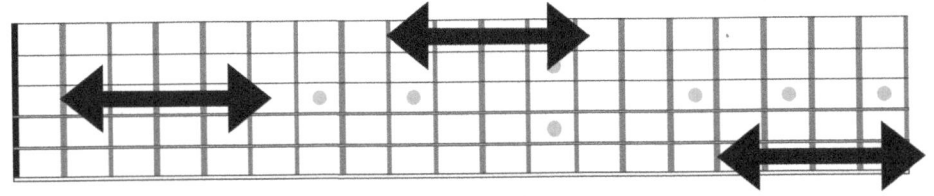

Now that you have an ascending version of horizontal movement under control, you should reverse this idea to unlock a descending horizontal movement, as demonstrated in **Ex.68**.

Ex.68 – *C# Minor Pentatonic (Descending Horizontal Movement)*

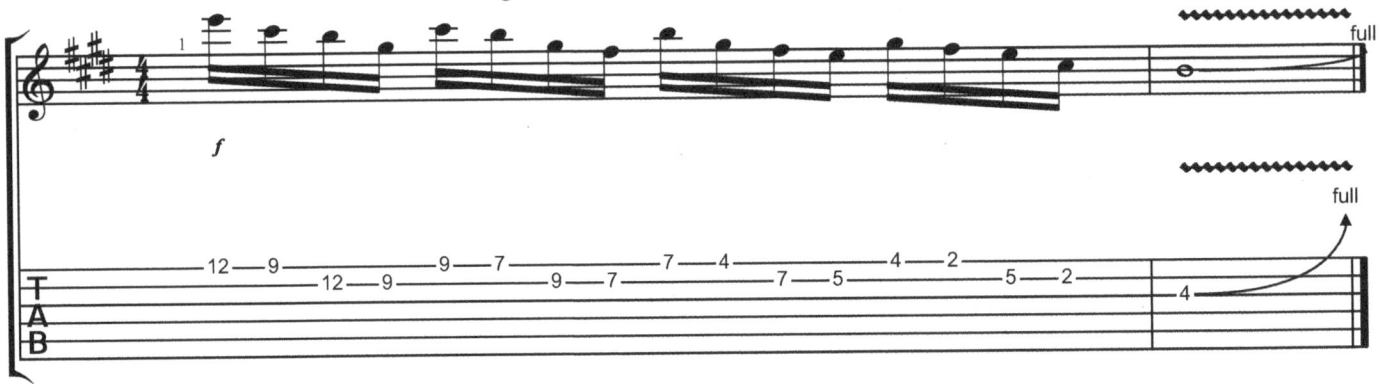

The next example introduces diagonal motion by ascending across the strings and up neck. Becoming comfortable with this directional motion may take your fingers and brain some additional practice and time to tackle this movement on the neck. Eventually, licks and ideas such as **Ex.69** will become comfortable to visualize and easier to perform.

Ex.69 – C# Minor Pentatonic (Diagonal Movement)

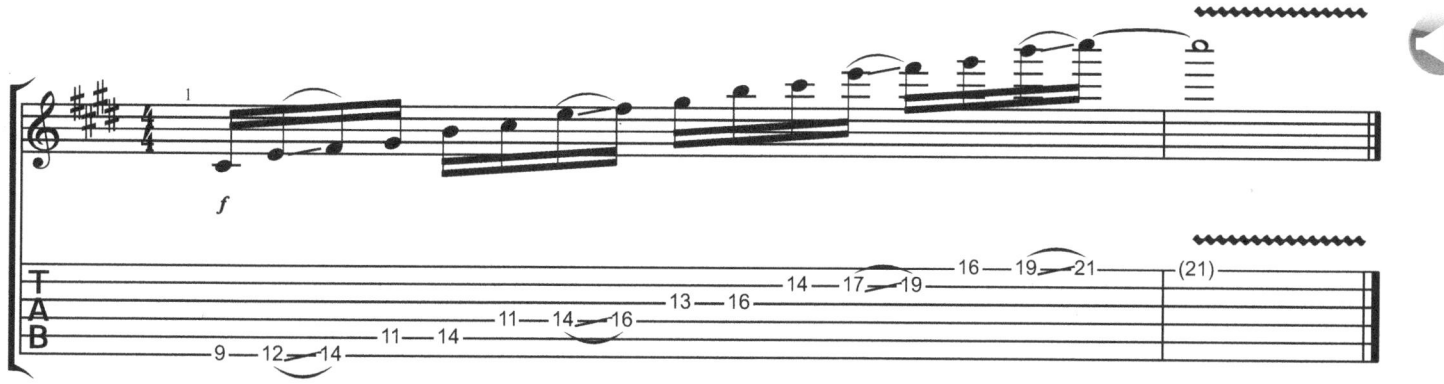

Fig.14 shares a fretboard diagram to help you visualize diagonal movement on the neck.

[Fig.14 – Diagonal Movement]

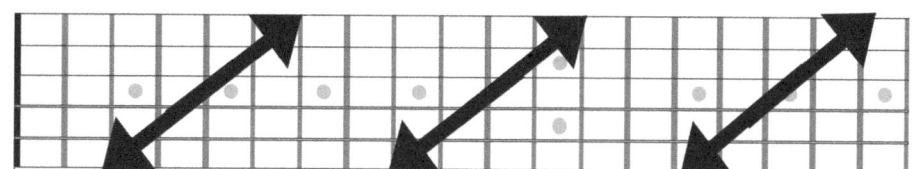

Now that you have ascending diagonal motion under your fingers, reverse this idea to perform descending diagonal phrases and licks. **Ex.70** will help you become acquainted with changing direction and creating additional licks and phrases based around this challenging movement on the neck.

Ex.70 – C# Minor Pentatonic (Descending Diagonal Movement)

The next example takes diagonal fretboard motion and completely reverses it to build ascending reverse-diagonal phrases. Reverse-diagonal position shifting and movement can be very confusing and challenging, so take your time practicing and exploring **Ex.71**.

Ex.71 – *C# Minor Pentatonic (Reverse-Diagonal Movement)*

Fig.15 provides a fretboard diagram to reveal reverse-diagonal movement on the neck.

[*Fig.15 – Reverse Diagonal Movement*]

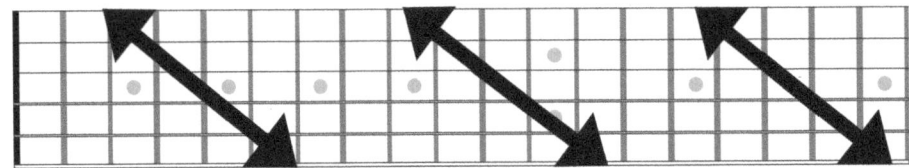

Ex.72 continues forward with reverse-diagonal movement, but reveals a descending reverse-diagonal variation. This example is the most challenging directional fretboard movement we've explored in this chapter, so spend additional time becoming familiar using this challenging frethand movement as it moves across the neck.

Ex.72 – *C# Minor Pentatonic (Descending Reverse-Diagonal Movement)*

To become more comfortable using direction-based movement on the neck with seven-note major and minor scales, **Ex.73** features a two-octave C# Aeolian scale and fingering, which is identical to the Aeolian scale (and fingering) discussed in the previous chapter, but shifted to the key of C# minor.

Ex.73 – *C# Aeolian*

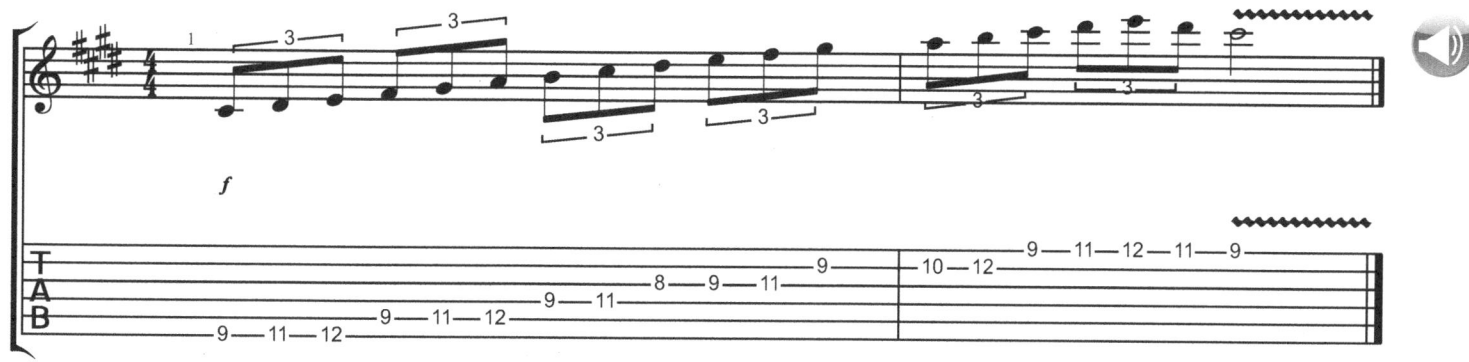

The next example recycles this vertical motion to create a smooth sounding legato lick, which might bring Joe Satriani or John Petrucci to mind. Practice **Ex.74** to get a feel for playing this scale using a diagonal fretboard movement while incorporating a slurred legato technique.

Ex.74 – *C# Aeolian (Vertical Movement)*

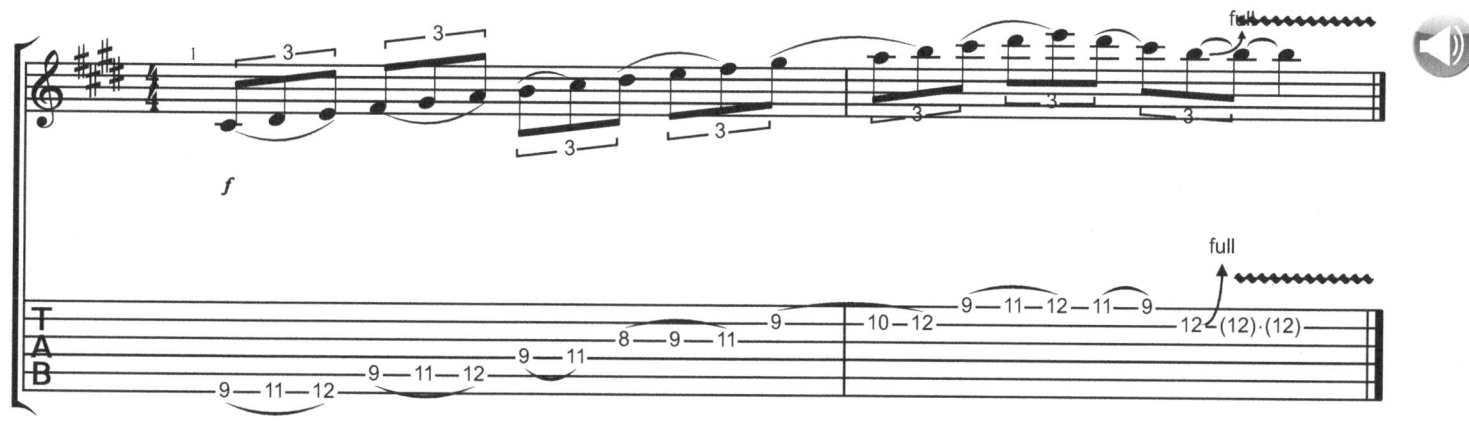

Ex.75 takes this scale and arranges the fingering along the neck to include horizontal movement on the fretboard. You can distinctly find this fretboard motion in the music of several guitar legends, including players such as Al Di Meola, Eddie Van Halen, and Steve Vai. For example, you can hear Eddie Van Halen using horizontal movement during his famous "Spanish Fly" guitar solo from *Van Halen II*.

Ex.75 – *C# Aeolian (Horizontal Movement)*

Moving forward, the next example shifts things into diagonal-based movement, as **Ex.76** features an example of ascending through this scale utilizing diagonal motion across the strings.

Ex.76 – C# Aeolian (Diagonal Movement)

The last variation of direction-based movement centers around reverse-diagonal fretboard movement on the neck and **Ex.77** shares a version of performing this motion.

Ex.77 – C# Aeolian (Reverse-Diagonal Movement)

The final section of this chapter includes string-skipped arpeggio shapes, which are quite popular with guitarists within a wide-range of musical styles. Many players associate this idea and sound with fleet-fingered players such as Paul Gilbert, John Petrucci, and Guthrie Govan, to name a few.

To begin, play through **Ex.78** which contains a string-skipped C# minor arpeggio. This two-note per-string fingering should be comfortable and somewhat familiar to Pentatonic-based players, yet the difficulty of this example centers around the noticeable intervallic stretch found within the fingering.

Ex.78 – *C# Minor Arpeggio (String-Skipped)*

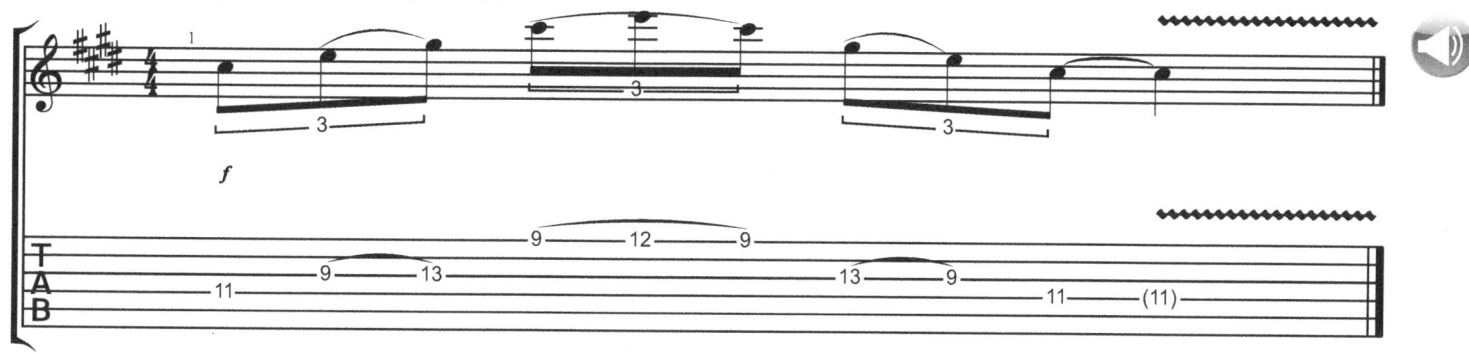

Now that you have this skipped fingering under your fingers, play through **Ex.79** to shift this arpeggio from the key of C# minor to the key of G# minor. Notice that we're maintaining a vertical motion on the fretboard for both of these arpeggios and creating a common i-v chord progression in C# minor.

Ex.79 – *C#m-G#m Arpeggio Progression (Vertical Movement)*

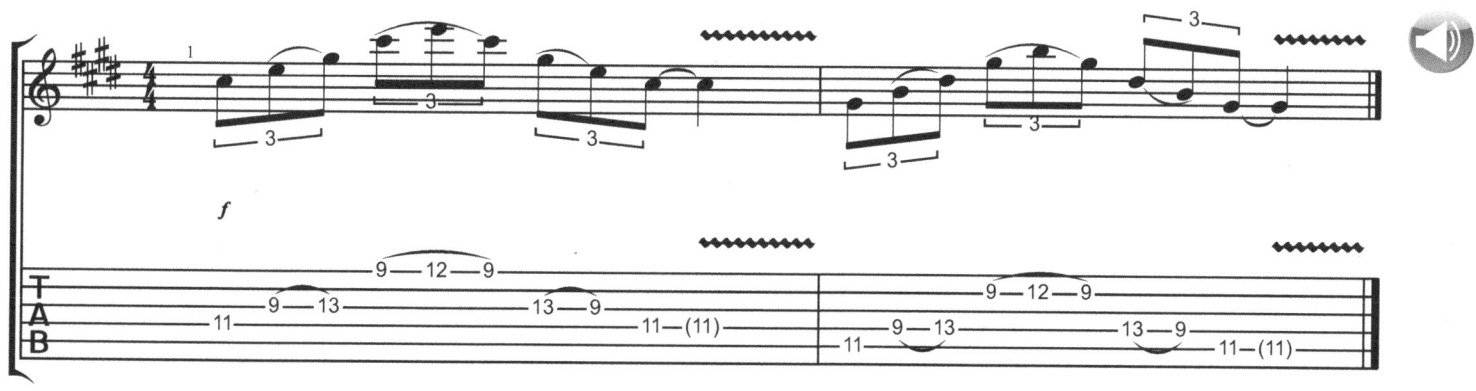

Ex.80 demonstrates how to take this skipped arpeggio and shifts the fingering downward using a horizontal motion. This movement converts the arpeggio from C# minor to Bb minor and uncovers a common i-bvii chord progression in the key of C# minor.

Ex.80 – *C#m-Bbm Arpeggio Progression (Horizontal Movement)*

The next example moves this concept forward by including diagonal movement for this string-skipped arpeggio. **Ex.81** demonstrates this idea by shifting C# minor to F# minor using diagonal motion and creates a very common i-iv chord progression.

Ex.81 – *C#m-F#m Arpeggio Progression (Diagonal Movement)*

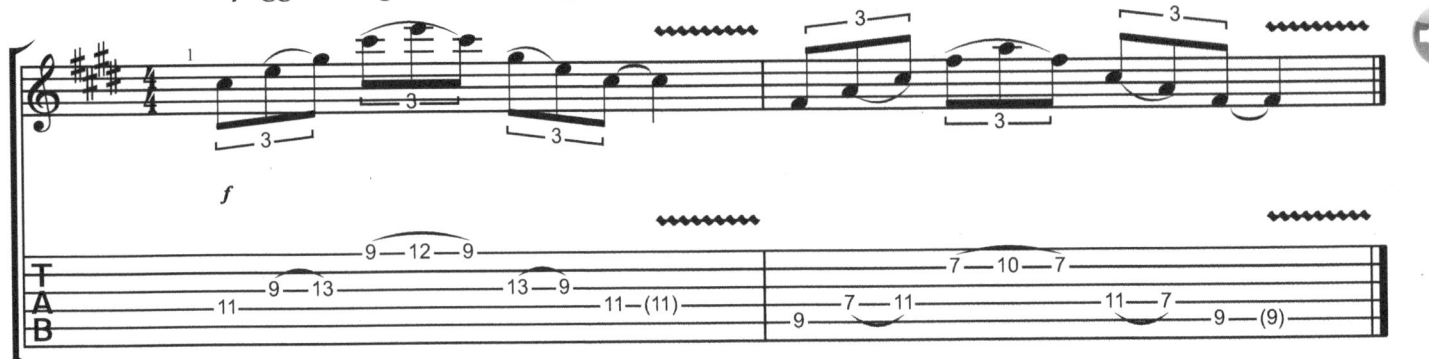

The next example reveals another version of reverse-diagonal motion and creates reverse-diagonal movement by shifting the arpeggio from C# minor to A major. Using **Ex.82** as a guide, you can discover additional ways of shifting string-skipped arpeggio shapes to other locations, keys, and groups of strings on the guitar.

Ex.82 – *C#m-A Arpeggio Progression (Diagonal Movement)*

The final example shares an extended string-skipping arpeggio workout that utilizes a combination of direction-based movement on the fretboard. **Ex.83** is in the style of shred-master Paul Gilbert and provides a great example of expanding this type of movement on the neck.

Ex.83 – *C#m-A-E-G# Arpeggio Progression (String-Skipped)*

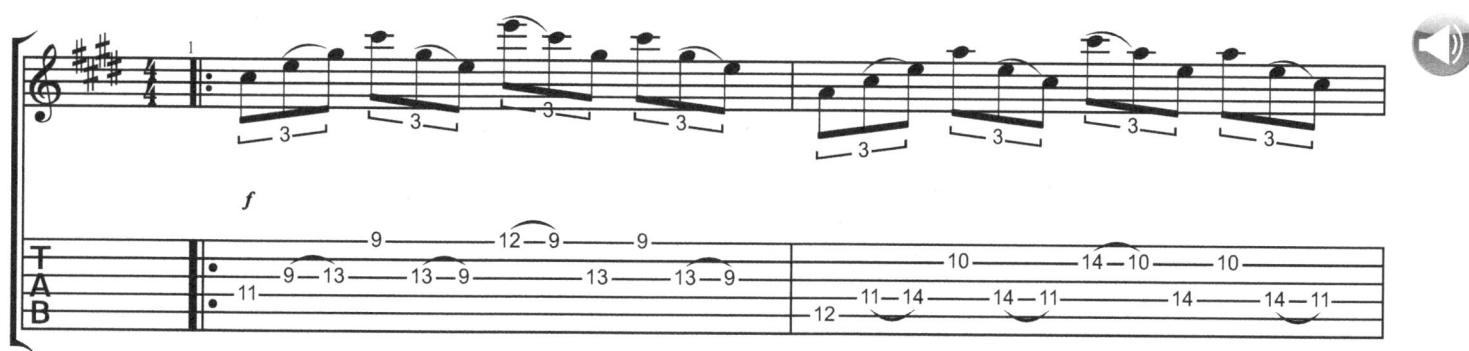

Now that you've arrived at the end of this book, you should continue expanding your awareness and knowledge of applying these and other shift-based ideas on the fretboard. This type of practice will not only expand your knowledge of the fretboard and the various position-shifting connections that exist, but you'll also improve your technique, shifting ability, and awareness of how to create new ideas and music in the future from recycled concepts and ideas. Good luck!

More Great Books from David Brewster...

MUTING THE GUITAR
00001199 Book/CD Pack..$19.99

ASAP GUITARIST GUIDE TO STRING BENDING & VIBRATO
00001347 Book/CD Pack..$19.99

GUITAR HARMONY FOR THE ROCK GUITARIST
00233915 Book/Online Audio.................................$19.99

TARGET TONES
00233322 Book/Online Audio.................................$19.99

You'll like what you hear!

P.O. Box 17878 - Anaheim Hills, CA 92817
(714) 779-9390   centerstrm@aol.com | www.centerstream-usa.com

More Great Guitar Books from Centerstream...

SCALES & MODES IN THE BEGINNING
by Ron Middlebrook

The most comprehensive and complete scale book written especially for the guitar. Chapers include: Fretboard Visualization • Scale Terminology • Scales and Modes • and a Scale to Chord Guide.
00000010..$11.95

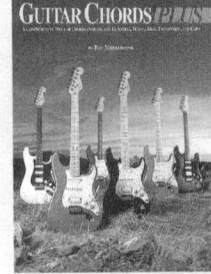

GUITAR CHORDS PLUS
by Ron Middlebrook

A comprehensive study of normal and extended chords, tuning, keys, transposing, capo use, and more. Includes over 500 helpful photos and diagrams, a key to guitar symbols, and a glossary of guitar terms.
00000011..$11.95

CELTIC CITTERN
by Doc Rossi

Although the cittern has a history spanning 500 years and several countries, like its cousin the Irish bouzouki, it is a relative newcomer to contemporary traditional music. Doc Rossi, a wellknown citternist in both traditional and early music, has created this book for intermediate to advanced players who want to improve their technique, develop ideas and learn new repertoire. Guitarists can play all of the tunes in this book on the guitar by tuning C F C G C F, low to high, and putting a capo at the second fret. The lowest line in the tablature then corresponds to the fifth string. The CD features all the tunes played at a medium tempo.
00001460 Book/CD Pack..$19.99

THE CHORD SCALE GUIDE
by Greg Cooper

The Chord Scale Guide will open up new voicings for chords and heighten your awareness of linear harmonization. This will benefit jazz ensemble players, rock guitarists and songwriters looking to create new and unique original music, and understand the harmony behind chords.
00000324..$15.95

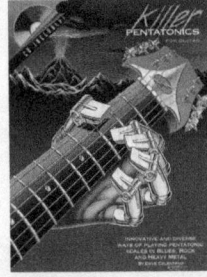

KILLER PENTATONICS FOR GUITAR
by Dave Celentano

Covers innovative and diverse ways of playing pentatonic scales in blues, rock and heavy metal. The licks and ideas in this book will give you a fresh approach to playing the pentatonic scale, hopefully inspiring you to reach for higher levels in your playing. The 37-minute companion CD features recorded examples.
00000285 Book/CD Pack..$19.95

IRISH YOU A MERRY CHRISTMAS
by Doug Esmond

This book includes Christmas melodies as well as lesserknown tunes from Scotland paired with seasonal titles. All the songs can be played solo or with other instruments. A CD is included with recordings of the author playing using both steel and nylon string guitars.
00001360 Book/CD Pack..$15.99

MELODY CHORDS FOR GUITAR
by Allan Holdsworth

Influential fusion player Allan Holdsworth provides guitarists with a simplified method of learning chords, in diagram form, for playing accompaniments and for playing popular melodies in "chord-solo" style. Covers: major, minor, altered, dominant and diminished scale notes in chord form, with lots of helpful reference tables and diagrams.
00000222..$24.95

MUTING THE GUITAR
by David Brewster

This book/CD pack teaches guitarists how to effectively mute anything! Author David Brewster covers three types of muting in detail: frethand, pickhand, and both hands. He provides 65 examples in the book, and 70 tracks on the accompanying CD.
00001199 Book/CD Pack..$19.99

P.O. Box 17878 - Anaheim Hills, CA 92817
(714) 779-9390   www.centerstream-usa.com

More Great Guitar Books from Centerstream...

ASAP POWER PICKING
For Electric and Acoustic Guitars

by David Brewster This book will help beginning guitarists "find" the strings of the guitar through a series of basic (yet melodic) picking exercises. As you become more comfortable striking the strings of the guitar with a pick using the exercises and examples here, you should eventually create your own variations and picking exercises.

00001330 Book/CD Pack $15.99

LATIN STYLES FOR GUITAR
by Brian Chambouleyron

A dozen intermediate to advanced originals in notes & tab display various Latin American styles. For each, the CD features the lead part as well as an accompaniment-only rhythm track for play along.

00001123 Book/CD Pack $19.95

GUITAR TUNING FOR THE COMPLETE MUSICAL IDIOT
by Ron Middlebrook

There's nothing more distracting than hearing a musician play out of tune. This user-friendly book/DVD pack teaches various methods for tuning guitars – even 12-strings! – and basses, including a section on using electronic tuning devices. Also covers intonation, picks, changing strings, and much more!

00000002 Book/DVD Pack...$16.95
00001198 DVD $10.00

ASAP CLASSICAL GUITAR
Learn How to Play the Classical Way
by James Douglas Esmond

Teacher-friendly or for self-study, this book/CD pack for beginning to intermediate guitarists features classical pieces and exercises presented progressively in notes and tab, with each explained thoroughly and performed on the accompanying CD. A great way to learn to play ASAP!

00001202 Book/CD Pack $15.95

THE COUNTRY GUITAR STYLE OF CHARLIE MONROE
Based on the 1936-1938 Bluebird Recordings by The Monroe Brothers
by Joseph Weidlich

This great overview of Charlie Monroe's unique guitar performance style (he used just his thumb and index finger) presents 52 songs, with an in-depth look at the backup patterns & techniques from each chord family (G, F, D, C, E, A), plus special note sequences, common substitutions and stock backup phrases. Includes the bluegrass classics "Roll in My Sweet Baby's Arms," "My Long Journey Home" and "Roll On, Buddy," plus a discography and complete Bluebird recording session info.
00001305 ....$19.99

ASAP GUITARIST GUIDE TO STRING BENDING & VIBRATO
Learn How to Bend the Correct Way
by Dave Brewster

String bending and vibrato are two of the most popular guitar techniques used in all musical styles, yet for most beginning and intermediate players, gaining control of them might seem overwhelming. This book outlines some of the most common bending and vibrato techniques and licks, teaching them in an easy-to-digest manner to help you see and hear how to use them with confidence in a musical context. Contains more than 150 helpful examples!
00001347 Book/CD Pack $19.99

HYMNS AND SPIRITUALS FOR FINGERSTYLE GUITAR
by James Douglas Esmond

Originating in the South during the antebellum days on the old plantations, at religious revivals and at camp meetings, hymns and spirituals are the native folk songs of our own America. This collection features 13 songs, some with two arrangements – one easy, the second more difficult. Songs include: Were You There? • Steal Away • Amazing Grace • Every Time I Feel the Spirit • Wade in the Water • and more.
00001183 Book/CD Pack $19.95

P.O. Box 17878 - Anaheim Hills, CA 92817
(714) 779-9390   www.centerstream-usa.com

The Original and Still the Best...

SCALES & MODES IN THE BEGINNING
by Ron Middlebrook
The most comprehensive and complete scale book written especially for the guitar. Chapers include: Fretboard Visualization, Scale Terminology, Scales and Modes, and a Scale to Chord Guide.
00000010..$11.99

P.O. Box 17878 - Anaheim Hills, CA 92817
(714) 779-9390 | www.centerstream-usa.com | centerstrm@aol.com

Another Great Book from Eddie Collins...

400 SMOKIN' BLUEGRASS GUITAR LICKS

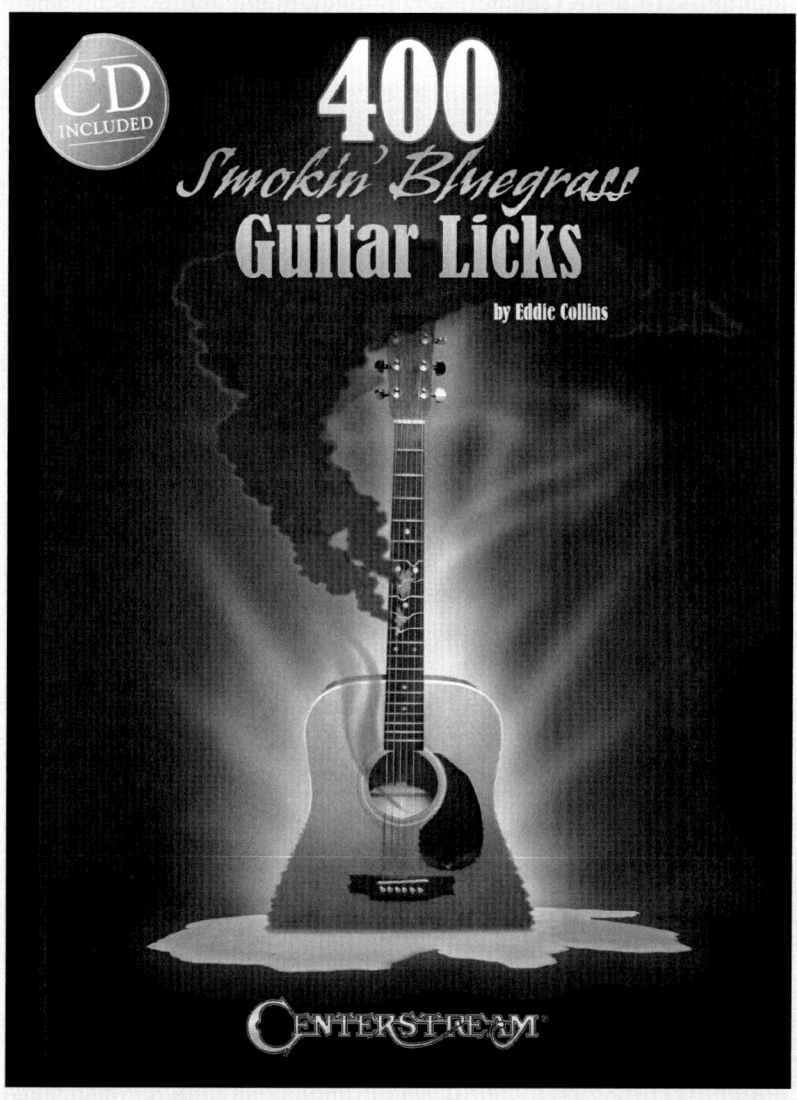

00123172..$19.99

P.O. Box 17878 - Anaheim Hills, CA 92817
(714) 779-9390   www.centerstream-usa.com